Praise for *Tales of a Country Parish*

'A luminous, lyrical book, brimming
with soul and the spirit of place.'

BISHOP ANDREW RUMSEY,
author of *English Grounds*

'Priests can make excellent chroniclers, having
privileged access as they do to the minds and
lives of others... *Tales of a Country Parish* is in
this brave tradition. Immensely knowledgeable
and curious, Colin Heber-Percy wears his
deep learning lightly and his reflections
are moving, compelling and insightful.'

PETER J. CONRADI,
author of *Iris Murdoch: A Life*

# TALES
# OF A
# COUNTRY
# PARISH

# TALES
# OF A
# COUNTRY
# PARISH

*From the vicar of Savernake Forest*
-
COLIN HEBER-PERCY

This paperback edition published in 2023

First published in 2022 by Short Books
an imprint of Octopus Publishing Group Ltd
Carmelite House, 50 Victoria Embankment
London, EC4Y ODZ
www.octopusbooks.co.uk

An Hachette UK Company
www.hachette.co.uk

10 9 8 7 6 5 4 3 2

A CIP catalogue record for this book is
available from the British Library.

ISBN: 978-1-78072-561-1

Cover design by Jo Walker
Interior design by Smith & Gilmour
Illustrations © Marina Strocchi

Printed and bound in Great Britain by Clays Ltd, Elcograf S.p.A

This FSC® label means that materials used for the
product have been responsibly sourced

And soft-headed clergy occasionally open the book of nature for us and read something that neither they nor their listeners understand.

Søren Kierkegaard

# CONTENTS

ONE SPRING MORNING LAST YEAR, in the hills behind the cottage where I live, I sat at the edge of a recently sown field of spring barley – a breath of green over the land's rising and falling – and I wept.

I'm a vicar. And when our churches were closed for worship on 17th March 2020 and then shut completely five days later, I wondered how I was supposed to carry on doing the job I love. I made phone calls to vulnerable and anxious parishioners; I volunteered (and volunteered my teenage children) to help with the local emergency food bank; I familiarised myself with offering worship online. But a vital part of any priestly ministry must be the day-to-day spiritual sustenance of souls in our care. Particularly when those souls are in distress, frightened, alone. So a daily email of reflection and prayer struck me as a good idea.

Good ideas are ignorable; necessity isn't.

And necessity has another, shorter name. In any life there are moments when the wriggle room runs out, when you know what's being asked of you. And by whom. Halfway along that track between two fields, circled by noisy lapwings, I ran into God. What are you doing here, Colin? (1 Kings 19.13).

You can wrestle; you'll lose.

I went home, pulled up a chair at the kitchen table, and started writing.

For many years I have lived in a corner of rural Wiltshire in southern England. Before becoming a priest, I worked as a screenwriter for the BBC, for Channel Four, and for independent production companies here in the UK, in Ireland, and in the States. But while my work took me all over the place, I always felt rooted here. The landscape – steep chalk downland and ancient forest – is criss-crossed with drovers' tracks and Anglo-Saxon *here-paths*, littered with megaliths, long barrows and flint quarries. The ancient past pokes through a patchwork of modern farmland, villages and market towns. My wife grew up here, and our children have never known another home. The places I write about are full of personal history: every tree, every bend in the lane, each dew pond, the gate on the top that whistles when the wind blows in from the east. I belong here. As much as this book is a record of a remarkable year, it's also a hymn to an ancient holy land.

'Hymn to a holy land' sounds carefully crafted and grand. But that couldn't be further from the truth. This book is a wall covered in bits of paper and chewing gum. Let me explain.

I learned the 'chewing gum method' many years ago from a philosophy professor whose advice I'd sought in desperation, unable to complete a long overdue piece of writing. 'Buy yourself a packet of gum,' she said, 'pop in a stick, chew, and start writing. No editing; just let the pen do the work. After exactly an hour – and it must be an hour, no more, no less – stop writing and stick the fruit of your labours up on the wall in front of you with the gum. The rest of the day is yours. Do that for four weeks, and you're done.'

This time I did it for a year.

Initially, I thought of the reflections as a way of meeting

a need in the people of the parishes. I hadn't recognised the need in myself. As I began to write, I quickly found the words that came were a sounding, a plummet dropped down into my own life, into my love of this place and its people. I wrote from the heart. Not for an audience or an editor, but for my friends.

At first the list of recipients was small; I knew them all. (I never think of them as *my* parishioners; I'm *their* vicar. It probably comes to the same thing but there's a world of difference in my head.) But then people began to forward the reflections, and the list of subscribers grew and grew. Under the circumstances, it doesn't seem quite right to say they went 'viral', but that's effectively what happened. Within a couple of weeks, they were being shared all over the world and I was receiving emails from people I'd never met living in places I'd never visited, or even heard of.

Many of their emails were deeply moving. A man wrote me from an intensive care unit where he was recovering from Covid; the hospital chaplain, he told me, read the reflections to him every morning by his bed. I exchanged emails with a parishioner's son, trapped and quarantining in a hotel room in Thailand; with an atheist living north of the Arctic Circle in Norway. He'd attach photos of his home under deep snow, and his first sight of the sun in six months. I received messages from a young man who was reading the reflections with his grandmother on Skype; they were a way of staying close, he said, when they couldn't be together. I was contacted by a Christian lady who was sharing the reflections and prayers with her Muslim neighbour, and she told me how they'd become friends during lockdown through the exchange of ideas. I had emails from Austria, from Georgia in the US, from South Africa and the Gulf, from the lonely, the frightened, the sick. I tried to reply to them all.

And all around me, in the villages and farming hamlets, the situation worsened. I had long conversations with parishioners wondering if they'd ever see their husbands again, or their wives, their mothers or fathers in care homes. I knew many who had to say goodbye for the last time through windows, sanitised hands pressed to the glass, tears behind Perspex face shields. I took funeral after funeral. Undertakers were overwhelmed.

And I just kept writing more or less on a wing and a prayer. Partly to keep a record, but more to keep in touch.

Fed up with video conferencing and mass-emailing apps, I tried to use the internet as little as possible during lockdown. Instead, when composing the reflections, I took to hunting down half-remembered quotes and passages from the pages of books in my untidy cottage and pulling long-loved records from foxed sleeves, blowing dust off scratched vinyl. My temporary desk at a window in my bedroom was a fortress of books, and the record player became a time machine.

The reflections were written over the course of twelve months, and it's the year's cycle that gives this book its structure: spring to spring. But laid over the familiar pattern of our changing seasons are less familiar spells of lockdown and quarantine, isolation, tiers and testing. For all of us, 2020 beat like the valves of a heart, closing and opening and closing.

The book can be read as a single narrative, the story of a 'plague year' as Daniel Defoe might have termed it, or as individual 'readings'. And by 'readings' I don't mean a lesson in church on Sunday; I mean 'readings' as in figures taken from a thermometer or blood pressure gauge, notes of vital signs made on a chart and left hooked onto a patient's hospital bed.

However you read *Tales of a Country Parish*, I hope you find something to nourish you. Although written from a Christian perspective, the reflections do not assume any faith in the reader. Religious faith, I believe, should never play the role of safe haven, or cosy club. Quite the reverse. As the Danish philosopher, Søren Kierkegaard (1813–1855) puts it, faith is 'not an easy matter… but the greatest and most difficult of all'. Through philosophy, music, poetry, personal anecdote and the sheer weirdness of ordained ministry, I set out partly to console and amuse, but also to explore, to stir things up a bit, to challenge and disrupt, perhaps even to disturb.

And remember, they're *reflections*. It's my belief that if we look carefully enough into our own hearts, lovingly enough at one another, and pay close enough attention to the world around us, we're able to glimpse in our reflections the Reflection in which we are all made.

> A man that looks on glass,
>    On it may stay his eye;
> Or if he pleaseth, through it pass,
>    And then the heav'n espy.
>
> 'The Elixir', George Herbert

## A NOTE ON THE TEXT

Rather than cluttering the book with footnotes, I decided to list at the back all the works I've quoted or consulted. If it's hard to find a particular reference, I apologise, but I can tell you, the list is a lot tidier than the shelves in my cottage.

Included with each of the original reflections was a link to a piece of music, something I'd dug out and to which I was listening as I wrote. Many of these (but not all) are very personal favourites; they have shaped me, inspired and consoled me over the years. At the end of each of the seasons – Spring, Summer, Autumn, Winter – I've given the tracks I shared at the time. Ideally, the music should go with the text, like a chilled Chablis with a dozen oysters, or a can of Irn-Bru with a sausage roll. All the music is easily available. And, for convenience, I've compiled them as a list on Spotify. Search for *Tales of a Country Parish*.

Here's the first. The night before my ordination, I listened to this at full volume on headphones in the empty cathedral. And I hope it stands now as an opening prayer: for you. Amen.

'Für Dich', Thomas Dinger, *Für Mich* (Telefunken, 1982)

# SPRING

TWO BUTTERFLIES are fluttering against the east window. Apart from me, they're the only living things in the place.

The stained glass, its boiled-sweet yellows, reds and blues, must look like freedom to the butterflies, and my closing hands a trap. But with the butterflies caged in my cupped palms, I walk down the aisle of All Saints' to the west door, and outside in the churchyard I open my hands to the spring sunshine.

It's Friday the 20th March 2020.

The butterflies twist and flicker up into the blue. They're like a prayer, and I haven't said a word.

This is the last time I'll set foot in church for months. When I do return, everything will have changed: the world, these parishes, me.

. . . . .

SITTING ON THE CHURCHYARD WALL the following Monday, I watch Joy, the churchwarden and organist, locking the door. Masked and self-conscious, we have a brief, socially distanced chat, unsure, both of us, whether we're even allowed to be here at all. And then she leaves me to sit alone in the sun with my thoughts.

Flint and stone and oak, All Saints' has been here since

the twelfth century. Looking up at the tower, I remember the girls at my primary school who told that story with their hands – here's a church, here's the steeple, through the doors and here are the people...

The churchyard is deserted, and so are the lanes and closes of the village behind me: where are the people?

Around the time those girls at my school were showing off their ability to tell stories with their hands, I became fascinated by a particular song which I've always associated with the church-people-steeple rhyme.

I can remember hearing and handling (and the handling is important) Mahalia Jackson's *Gospels, Spirituals & Hymns* for the first time. There was an old Garrard turntable, size of a suitcase, sitting under the window in my grandfather's study. The room smelled of pipe smoke, beeswax, and Irish wolfhound. Quad amps and huge Tannoy speakers squatting in the corners of the room, all polished wood and textured mesh. His record collection, arranged, sleeveless, in a wire rack, was limited to marches played by the band of the Coldstream Guards, recordings of steam trains and – unlikely though it sounds – gospel music. I had a soft spot for the Radetzky March, I admit, but Mahalia was my favourite from first play. I loved the hiss and crackle as the needle dropped onto vinyl or shellac, and running my hands over the mesh while the music was playing, feeling the throb of it under my fingers.

He's got the whole world in his hands, she sang.

His hands would have to be very big, I thought. Big as Grandpa's. Bigger even. And as clever as the hands of the girls at my school. Here's a church, steeple, parson; here are the people.

Fresh in my mind this morning as I sit on the wall in the spring sunshine, are images, shaky mobile phone footage of a completely empty urban environment. Streets deserted. Airports and supermarkets desolate. As Lent draws to a close we'll be reading again those verses from Lamentations:

> How lonely sits the city
> that once was full of people.
>
> Lamentations 1.1

The footage from Wuhan could be those lines brought to life, or death. But in fact both the verse and the footage are misleading: cities can't be lonely (or seated for that matter); and Wuhan isn't empty. It's just that the wrists haven't twisted, the palms haven't been opened to reveal all the people inside. Our cities, towns and villages are full of people. But they're trapped, fearful in their homes, waiting for the story to start again.

What I sense when I look at those images from Wuhan or at the locked door of All Saints' is how we may need, over the coming months, to reimagine our ways of being cities, towns, villages, churches. Perhaps we need to think of them less as places, and more as stories. They are stories unfolding around us with ourselves as a vital part.

In the years running up to 2012, large portions of the East End of London were redeveloped in preparation for the city's hosting of the Olympic Games. In charge of the process was Lord Coe. I remember listening to Coe on a radio phone-in being taken to task by a caller who said her neighbourhood park was being bulldozed to make room for Olympic facilities. Coe pointed out that after the redevelopment there would be more 'ecologically managed green space' in the neighbourhood than there had been previously; the city would be greener. The caller responded by saying, 'I'm not talking about ecologically managed green space; I'm talking about our park. Where I grew up, where I used to play as a child, and where I take my children to play now.' Missing from 'ecologically managed green space' is *story*.

This notion of story presents us with an opportunity, I think, a chance to see ourselves as characters in an unfolding narrative, people of a story, belonging to it like fingers to a hand. We need to inhabit the story in the way the Hebrews inhabited the Exodus story, learning from it, growing through it and allowing ourselves to be changed by it: to become the people we are called to be. It may not be a reassuring story. It may not have a happy ending, but it's ours. Or rather, we are its.

The French philosopher Gilles Deleuze (1925–1995) urges us, 'To become worthy of what happens to us, to become the offspring of one's own events, and thereby to be reborn... and to break with one's carnal birth'. The veiled reference in that final phrase is to John 3.1–8 where Jesus tells Nicodemus he must be born again, this time not of the flesh, but of the Spirit. I think part of what Jesus means is that we're called to be 'worthy of what happens to us', worthy of being characters in an unfolding drama, emerging *from* it and belonging *to* it. God is not the storyteller; God is the story.

.....

THE ROOM WHERE I'M WRITING – and I'm writing early this morning – is heavily, almost overpoweringly scented with lilac. Sprays of pink and purple and white in a jug on the table beside me. Lilac grows everywhere around here, in the chalky gathers and pleats under the downs, around ponds, and edging kitchen gardens.

For the first time in weeks, it's raining and everything is reviving. After the heat of the last few days, the sound of water dripping from a broken gutter and the draughts of cold air from a window left open upstairs are refreshing, welcome.

My copy of *The Practice of the Presence of God* by Brother Lawrence (1614–1691), a lay brother in a Carmelite monastery outside Paris, was given me by my grandmother on my confirmation. The majority of the little book comprises letters by Lawrence to various correspondents who have written asking for spiritual guidance and advice. But prefacing the letters are transcripts of conversations between Lawrence and an unnamed interlocutor. The first conversation begins like this:

> In the winter, seeing a tree stripped of its leaves, and considering that within a little time the leaves would be renewed, and after that the flowers and fruit appear, [Brother Lawrence] received a high view of the providence and power of GOD, which has never since been effaced from his soul.

Easy to have a high view of the providence and power of God this spring. There's a stand of beeches, high on the downs, where I often go to say Morning Prayer. The path leading to the spot is overgrown with hazels, brambles and holly, but then it opens out suddenly. It's like entering a cathedral: the grey shafts of the beeches either side, and above, the vaulting, a bright lattice of emerald and jade.

Each spring, spring itself seems to stand in need of explanation. And demands a thanksgiving. But Brother Lawrence's high view of the providence and power of God doesn't derive from the beauty or pleasantness of creation in spring, rather from its startling abundance. Just a few weeks ago – when Covid was still only a news item – I stood with Gareth, the farm manager, who was using a loader to ferry half-ton buckets of spring barley up onto the tops for sowing. Now, the rolls and rucks of the brown fields are shot with green, and the grassy banks are covered with columbines. Here and there, in the shade, are fragrant clumps of wild garlic. How could you possibly have guessed three months ago that those bare winter branches would be bent under blossom, the hedgerows hazy with new growth? Most remarkable of all, it seems to me, are the candles on a horse chestnut tree. It's not their beauty, actually, that strikes you. Almost the opposite. They're like those Murano glass chandeliers: too much, over the top. They are the dandy and disreputable cousins to the lilac blooms in front of me.

How are we to respond to the sheer profligacy of creation? We could try to understand creation in two ways: by taking it to bits, testing it, examining it under the cold lamp of reason. So, horse chestnut panicles have an evolutionarily established function, are a genetically determined expression of the organism's life cycle; they have a place in our taxonomy, an explanation. Or we could try to understand by *standing under*, standing under the candling tree, and just looking up in wonder. The honey-hum of bees in the sunshine, the feel of rain on our faces this morning, dripping in the new leaves.

Both forms of understanding are vital and valid. Yet, perhaps inevitably, these different approaches have seen themselves as mutually exclusive. Keats famously draws up the battle lines in his poem *Lamia*, written in 1819:

> Do not all charms fly
> At the mere touch of cold philosophy?
> There was an awful rainbow once in heaven:
> We know her woof, her texture; she is given
> In the dull catalogue of common things.
> Philosophy will clip an Angel's wings,
> Conquer all mysteries by rule and line,
> Empty the haunted air, and gnomèd mine—
> Unweave a rainbow...

Keats's cold philosophy assumes a conquering position – outside nature, outside creation. Without warrant, it claims transcendence and brings its impressive capacity for analysis to bear on all before it, failing in the process to see itself in the mix, in the swim of things. It will clip an angel's wings, unweave a rainbow and offer the results as answers. When John Ruskin (1819–1900) studies a thistle-top, he chooses not to do so through a microscope. 'Flowers,' he says, 'like everything else that is lovely in the visible world, are only to be seen rightly with the eyes which the God who made them gave us.' This isn't, I think, to deny the usefulness of a microscope; it's simply to point out that utility isn't always a criterion of value, let alone loveliness.

Stand, like Brother Lawrence, under a beech tree in winter, its black branches a lung flayed by the west wind; stand there till spring as the tree comes into leaf, life rising through it like mercury through a thermometer; and when summer comes with a crown, bow to the tree's demands for our shaded obeisance, until autumn gales strip its leaves in rude whirls. And never let that 'high view' be effaced from your soul.

.....

HOW FAR CAN I WALK, run or ride my bike in order to take my daily exercise? If I drive forty minutes to stand on an empty beach, am I breaking the law? Do replacement washers for a dripping tap count as 'necessary items'? All these questions are suddenly put aside. My wife, Emma, has taken to her bed with a dry cough, fever, exhaustion. I bring her meals which she can't taste and paracetamols which make no difference and I top up the jug of water on her bedside table. And wash my hands till they're raw. A call to the NHS helpline; we go through a checklist of symptoms, and it's clear Emma has the virus. Perhaps she picked it up at the primary school where she works. Our teenage children – Joey, Theo and Aggie – are anxious. What was an item on the news is now among us, inside us. Sometimes I think we listen to the news not to keep up with events, but to keep them at bay. News has a magical, prophylactic function: if it's on the news, it's somehow hived off, over there. Now it's here; we *are* the news.

Yesterday I took a phone call from someone at Wiltshire

Council who asked me how much spare capacity there is in the graveyards and cemeteries of the parishes I look after. 'We may well need all that space,' the council official explained, 'as overspill from larger conurbations.' Overspill – the word haunts me.

At the beginning of Lent, I made my usual 'no alcohol' resolution. But pandemic is penitence enough, I think. So, on his eighteenth birthday, in the midst of all the mayhem, Theo mixes us both Old Fashioneds, and we go and stand at the gate to the field behind our cottage, watching the sun tuck itself into the Vale of Pewsey. It's not the eighteenth birthday he'd imagined, but he's gracious enough not to complain. We'll have a party when all this is over, I promise him, when Mum's better. But it sounds hollow, even as I say the words. When all this is over. I have a suspicion it's hardly started.

Back in the kitchen, Aggie's unimpressed with my cauliflower curry. (Since Emma fell ill, we've been relying on what's left in the larder and veg box deliveries from the Swan, our local pub, now a life support machine.) Talking of the pub, Aggie tells me she's longing for a rare steak and a bowl of chips. We've already had tears this morning at the prospect of weeks without Quavers or tiramisu.

I fear she may have sent up a distress signal because this afternoon I found my colleague, Rev'd Jo, coming up the path with China, her elderly Staffordshire bull terrier trundling along breathlessly behind her. Jo has brought an emergency delivery of Italian dessert and pillow-sized bags of thermo-mechanically extruded potato starch snacks. Masked, she puts the gifts down on the path and stands back as we approach. 'I was hungry and you gave me food'

(Matthew 25.35). Not entirely sure this is what Jesus had in mind, but Aggie's thrilled. She bursts into tears, and tucks in immediately.

Experimenting with worship on a video-conferencing platform later that night, Jo leads our prayers, with China snoring away in the background. It's strangely calming. Still, Aggie's tears are infectious, and I hope no one can see my shoulders shaking. In the end, I splodge Blu-Tack over the laptop camera, and weep.

......

AT ORDINATION, and on being licensed to a parish, a new priest swears oaths to obey the bishop and the queen, and promises to abide by the canons of the Church of England and the Thirty-Nine Articles. I don't have a problem with any of this. The bishop is close by and kind. The queen is far away and can't chop off my head. And I love the Church, despite its best efforts sometimes.

But the schoolboy lurks in the background still. And if I'm honest, the passages in scripture that continue to give me pause always relate to obedience and submission. 'Obey your leaders and submit to them, for they are keeping watch over your souls, as those who will have to give an account' (Hebrews 13.17). To me, this smacks of the headmaster's study. And you won't be surprised to learn Psalm 119 isn't a personal favourite: statutes, ordinances, commandments, laws and on and on.

Many years ago, I spent time in the Greek Orthodox monasteries of Mount Athos in Greece. I was travelling with several companions, one of whom was my brother-in-law, Johnny. I don't think Johnny would mind my saying he was there less as a pilgrim and more as a chaperone for his father, George. George had served in Greece during the Second World War, fighting with British Special Forces behind enemy lines alongside the ferocious Greek resistance, the Sacred Squadron. He was the first British officer to enter Athens, on a bicycle, as the Germans retreated. Thronging Syntagma Square, the liberated Athenians chanted his name until he appeared on a balcony of the Grand Bretagne Hotel to jubilant cheering. For George, towards the end of his life, visiting Athos represented a final crown, a hallowed farewell to a country that honoured him as a hero. (And the Greeks know a thing or two about heroes.) Years later, after George's memorial service at the Anglican church in Athens, I remember one old veteran of the Sacred Squadron telling me how George 'had balls of steel' and he made a gesture with his hands. 'The bravest man I ever met,' he said, tears in his eyes.

The Holy Mountain, as the Greeks think of Athos, is closer to Heaven than Earth. You leave for the mountain by ferry from a village called Ouranopolis: sky town. This is space travel.

Life in the monasteries, particularly during Lent when we were visiting, is austere, tough. Simple at the best of times, the food dwindles to meagre. Olives, bread, water. And the round of prayer is gruelling. In one monastery, George got into an argument with the abbot on the subject of Dostoevsky. George dared to express a preference for Tolstoy. The abbot stared at him, aghast. Balls of steel, George stood his ground. The abbot had no English, and George no Greek, so French was (literally) the *lingua franca*. In a rumbling bass from behind his beard, the abbot said, '*Mais Dostoevsky, il est le plus profond.*' George shrugged, '*Trop profond pour moi.*'

Every morning at three o'clock we were woken by the resonant banging of the semandron, our call to liturgy, to prayer. In his eighties, impeccably turned out in a Campbell's of Beauly cashmere cardigan, straight-backed and clean shaven, George would stand for three hours of worship in the candlelit *katholikon*. Clinging to the shadows, Johnny and I slumped against the misericords like scarecrows, and slept.

For Johnny, monastic life quickly palled. I remember him describing one of the more affluent monasteries as a gilded cage; the less well-off establishments, they were just cages.

Half-starved, Johnny would lead some of us on trips to the one taverna on the peninsula. We'd order spanakopita and Heinekens. 'Brother Johnny's Little Treats', we called them, a little unfairly because we *all* appreciated those post-trapeza trips to the 'pub', walking an hour or more along steep, rough tracks in search of beer and food.

At silent mealtimes in the monasteries a bell would ring and you could sit. Another bell and you could begin eating. Then after a few minutes a third bell was the signal to stop eating and stand. I remember one meal – thin broth, a tasteless bean stew and a baklava. Knowing I didn't have long between bells, I bypassed the unappetising savouries and went straight for the baklava. It was as delicious as it looked, dripping with honey. Johnny, however, politely ploughed his way through broth and beans, and was just coming to the baklava, first mouthful poised between plate and lip, when the bell rang and he had to drop his mouthful back on the plate.

Everyone stood, and during a closing prayer I signalled Johnny to drop his paper napkin over the baklava and sur-reptitiously pocket it for later. As the abbot began to march down the room, Johnny made his move, grabbed the baklava under the napkin. But it was honey-stuck fast to the thin metal plate underneath; he couldn't pocket pud-ding *and* plate. Terrified, he dropped the lot. An awful clatter of metal on marble in the silence.

The abbot stopped, turned and gave Johnny the full Psalm 119 stare.

After that, he'd had enough. While I adored my time on the Holy Mountain, Johnny couldn't wait to get away, fed up with the ritual and the rules. He yearned for freedom.

When the Pharisees declare to Jesus that they are Abraham's children and have always been free (John 8.33), they're forgetting their own foundational story – liberation from slavery in Egypt. St Paul is playing on these ideas when he tells the Galatians to 'Stand firm and do not be subject again to the yoke of slavery' (Galatians 5.1). Johnny would agree with that. He certainly saw his time on Athos as 'Egypt', all the rules as a yoke of slavery. But for Paul, freedom is not simply the absence of constraint. He makes a radical further claim. 'We are members of one another,' (Ephesians 4.25), and 'subject to one another' (Ephesians 5.21). Freedom, as Christians understand the term, is not an unrestricted right to choose for ourselves, nor a set of individual liberties to be defended at all costs from the col-lective or the culture or the state. Or the abbot. No, Christian liberty is an expression of mutual interdepend-ence. It is freedom in and through belonging to one another. Christians are subject to one another, members of one another as the body of Christ.

The truth is, I saw this freedom in Johnny's loving commitment to his father. And in George's growing reliance on his son.

There's a sorry coda to the story of our trip to Mount Athos. Exuberant at having left the Holy Mountain, Johnny overdid it in the harbour bars of Thessaloniki on our first night of 'freedom'. After a fracas in one particular establishment, he was carted away to the police cells to cool off.

Like Saints Paul and Silas in Philippi just a few miles down the road and a couple of millennia earlier, Johnny was banged up in northern Greece, somewhat unfairly. No miraculous freeing in the middle of the night for Johnny, as there was for the apostles (Acts 16.11–40). Instead, in the morning, an irate George had to go and bail his battered boy from jail. Trained under the Colonels, the Greek police are not the gentlest or most considerate hosts. Johnny bore the scars for weeks from the cable ties they used to bind his wrists.

. . . . .

AFTER A FORTNIGHT IN BED, Emma turns a corner. She's up, weak and coughing all the time, but able to sit in the sunshine; she's even begun planting out seedlings from the greenhouse. And now that she's able to join us for supper – more cauliflower curry – at the kitchen table, she's noticing a 'little' problem to which I've been trying to turn a blind eye all the time she's been in bed. There are mice everywhere.

'See what happens when I'm not around? What would you do if I'd died or was in intensive care?' A bit melodramatic, I think, but the truth is, I know I'd have gone to pieces. To be honest, I was pretty much in pieces anyway. Just for the moment, I'm prepared to do anything she says.

This is an old house full of holes and gaps and cavities, a roof of wooden shingles and walls covered in ivy: we may as well hang up a 'vacancies' sign. 'Overrun' sounds biblical, but it's the word Emma used. A state of emergency is declared.

'Do you think we should get a cat?' I ask.

'With your allergies?'

And so I find myself scanning a selection of traps and poisons in the one hardware shop that has remained open in lockdown. Confronted by the array of lethal-looking devices, I begin to feel uneasy. Names like *Jawz*, *Snappies* and *Tomcat*, all advertising clean kills and easy disposal. This doesn't seem right at all. In *Leaves of Grass*, Walt Whitman tells us 'a mouse is miracle enough to stagger sextillions of infidels'. And here I am, plotting ways to break their miraculous little necks. I ask advice of the shopkeeper. He notices the dog collar, smiles. 'What would St Francis do?'

I leave with an armful of expensive 'humane' traps, more sucker than saint. Emma is furious. But actually, these non-lethal traps have proved quite effective. Every morning I find mice scrabbling about in the little clear plastic boxes I've baited with peanut butter the night before. On my way to making food bank deliveries, or pastoral visits in parishioners' gardens, I release the mice in a nearby field or copse. It feels illicit somehow. There's a

Cold War quality to these surreptitious 'drops'.

And then I start to wonder, as I drive along, how humane are these traps really? I mean, what must it be like to be a mouse trapped inside a clear plastic box on the backseat of my Seat Ibiza? Frightening and disorientating, judging from their movements. Fair enough. But that's not really an answer to my question; we have no way of knowing what it feels like to be frightened or disorientated *as a mouse*. I can imagine the confusion, the claustrophobia. But it's *my* confusion, *my* sense of claustrophobia. (Actually, if you want to remind yourself what confusion and claustrophobia feel like, you could do a lot worse than just sit in a Seat Ibiza for five minutes.)

My point is, we only know what it's like to be us; and we only know the world as it appears to us. Immanuel Kant (1724–1804) formalised this idea in *The Critique of Pure Reason*. It's a simplistic reading, I'm sure, but I've always understood Kant's transcendental aesthetic to mean, essentially, that human beings can only ever experience the world under conditions that are peculiar to human beings. Our desire to know what the world might look like from a mouse's standpoint, or a Martian's, or from no particular standpoint at all can never be satisfied. This is how Friedrich Nietzsche (1844–1900) puts it in *The Joyous Science*:

> We cannot look around our own corner; it is hopeless curiosity to want to know what other forms of intellect and perspectives might exist.

I don't think any curiosity is hopeless. Almost by definition, curiosity is hopeful. But I know what Nietzsche means. When I wonder how the mouse feels, I can only ever imagine in the palette of feelings available to me. The mousetrap brings man and mouse into unlikely communion on the back seat of my car, but it only serves to demonstrate how actual communion is impossible. We can't step outside ourselves. In a way, we're as trapped as the mouse, just on the other side of the clear plastic box.

Nietzsche's thoughts on this matter, though revolutionary in 1882, were not remotely new and had thoroughly Christian credentials. Writing in the fourth century, bishop and theologian Gregory of Nyssa makes this perfectly Nietzschean (and Kantian) point in a sermon on Ecclesiastes:

> The whole of creation is unable to stand outside of itself by means of an intuitive knowing grasp, but always remains within itself; and whatever it sees, it sees only itself, and if it believes it sees something beyond itself – well, it is not of its nature to see beyond itself.

In short, the whole of creation is a Perspex box. Does that make it a trap? Precisely not. Gregory's thinking (and Nietzsche's unintentionally) sheds light on the deep meaning of one of the most misunderstood and misused moments of scripture:

> Then God said, 'Let us make humankind in our image, according to our likeness'... So God created humankind in his image, in the image of God he created them.
>
> Genesis 1.26–27

Forget the fancy words like 'humankind', 'image', 'created' for a moment, because it's the 'in' that counts here. To be created in the image of God doesn't mean we are *like* God. It means we live and move and have our being *in* the image of God. The image is our box, our context, our horizon. To be alive at all is to be in him. Does that feel like a trap?

Honestly? Yes, sometimes. We're human, all too human. But it's a trap like my hands around the butterflies were a trap, like these plastic boxes are a trap, like Athos is a trap: some traps are openings into a freedom we can't even imagine.

I release the catch and open the lid, and then with a flick of the tail, the mouse leaps and disappears into the grass and is gone.

.....

IT'S WALKING SEASON. We're in Rogationtide, the time of year when we steer a parallel course with our pagan ancestors and ask God's blessing on our crops for a bountiful harvest. One of the ancient traditions associated with Rogation is the beating of the parish boundaries, circumnavigating the limits of our little patch of creation. So, yesterday afternoon, I walked for hours in the spring sunshine with Nick, a friend since our children were babies. I have photos of Joey with Nick's twin daughters, Isla and Maisie, on their first morning at playgroup, and another of them in a paddling pool together, grinning toothlessly. And a few years later, Isla gave Joey his first Valentine's: a CD of *The Rise and Fall of Ziggy Stardust and the Spiders from Mars*. Soul love, truly.

Writing in the seventeenth century, George Herbert (1593–1633), the English poet and priest, called the beating of the bounds: 'procession'. He acknowledges the custom's pre-Christian roots but – ever practical – comes down in their favour, nonetheless, albeit after some judicious and paternalistic paring:

> The Country Parson is a lover of old customs if they are good and harmless; and the rather, because country people are much addicted to them, so that to favour them therein is to win their hearts, and to oppose them therein is to deject them. If there be any ill in the custom that may be severed from the good, he pares the apple, and gives them the clean to feed on.

Herbert's *The Country Parson*, from which the above is a quote, is his 'how to' manual for rural parish ministry. Easily weathering ill-conceived modern swipes, it is still a richly valuable and kindly companion. Chapter thirty-five is called 'The Parson's Condescending'. Let them get away with these 'old customs', Herbert is saying, so long as they're harmless and you can win your parishioners round thereby. More cynical than condescending perhaps? But Herbert didn't have a cynical bone in his body. And anyway, what's wrong with condescension? It just means 'descending with'. So, Herbert is only following Christ's example and being *with* those he's called to love and care for. The Incarnation is a cosmic condescension.

Walking with his parishioners, Herbert goes on to detail what it is about the practice of procession he thinks beneficial:

There are contained therein four manifest advantages: first, a blessing of God for the fruits of the field; secondly, justice in the preservation of bounds; thirdly, charity in loving walking and neighbourly accompanying one another, with reconciling of differences at that time, if there be any; fourthly, relieving the poor by a liberal distribution and largess, which at that time is, or ought to be used.

On our walk yesterday afternoon, Nick and I were blessed, surrounded by skylarks haunting the high ground, by clouds of may in the hedgerows, buttercups on the banks and bluebells through the woods. And we heard our first cuckoo.

Did we police the border, ensure the just preservation of boundaries? I'm currently unaware of any incursions from hostile neighbouring parishes, so this 'manifest advantage' we could safely set aside. But imagine places where the parish boundary is your house, your front room, your heart. Where practising your faith – whatever faith – is dangerous, disallowed, where worship is forbidden, blasphemy laws a bludgeon. That's my rogation, my asking today: for religious tolerance.

Together, Nick and I certainly took joy in a 'neighbourly accompanying of one another' and there were no differences to be reconciled, only laughter and stories shared. He showed me a news item on his phone. Isla, is in Manchester studying for a psychology degree. She is one of the students penned into their accommodation and under police guard. If you peer closely enough, you can just see Isla in the background of some of the footage.

Nick's laughing. But he misses her.

Separation, isolation has been painful for us all. I drove to see my parents on Saturday. No hugs or kisses, but presence. Actual physical presence, at last. 'Absence breeds strangeness,' Herbert writes further on in the same chapter, 'but presence love.'

And largess, the fourth of Herbert's advantages? I see this every Monday and Friday morning when people come to the food bank we've set up in the Church Centre. Herbert probably wouldn't recognise Fray Bentos pies or cartons of UHT milk or pot noodles as fruits of the field, but he'd know generosity and neighbourliness when he saw it.

The other day, Ralph knocked on my door. An electrician, parishioner and old friend, Ralph had managed to pick up a toaster, a kettle and a table lamp, all in good working order, which were going to be thrown out. 'For your boy, vicar,' he said, 'when he goes off to university in the autumn.'

Ralph had been doing some work at a cottage down the road. Flint Cottage was bought in the 1940s by Dr Makower, an economics don at Oxford who was serving, at the time she bought the cottage, in Churchill's S-Branch, an elite group of academic statisticians and economists. After the war, she worked as a missionary, smuggling crates and crates of Bibles into Mao's China. She died long before my time here but her cottage, which now belongs to her two nephews, has never been modernised or altered; it's a shrine to their aunt, full of books and fossils, a grand piano and a record player with stacks of jazz albums. I wish I'd known her.

Our walk takes us back into the village through the garden of Dr Makower's cottage, past the swing from an old sycamore which Nick remembers Isla's twin sister, Maisie used to love. And here, unexpectedly, we're joined by a cat who follows us all the way back up the lane, and miaows outside our cottage door for the rest of the day. In the end, I take pity and let her in. On making enquiries, I discover she comes from the next village, a mile or so away over the hill. But when Aggie contacts the owners they don't seem particularly concerned or in any hurry to have her returned. So, in spite of Emma's protests, the cat ends up in the kitchen, eating leftovers from our fish pie and staying the night.

Rogation. Ask, and you're liable to end up with more than you bargained for.

I don't bother with mousetraps tonight.

.....

AT THE END OF THE FIRST WORLD WAR, Helen Turrell travels to northern France to put flowers on the grave of her illegitimate son, Michael, one of the fallen. To those travelling with her, she describes Michael as her 'nephew'.

This is the simple, touching basis of a short story by Rudyard Kipling (who had lost his own son during that conflict). The story ends:

> A man knelt behind a line of headstones – evidently a gardener, for he was firming a young plant in the soft earth. She went towards him, her paper in her hand.

He rose at her approach and without prelude or salutation asked: 'Who are you looking for?'

'Lieutenant Michael Turrell – my nephew,' said Helen slowly and word for word, as she had many thousands of times in her life.

The man lifted his eyes and looked at her with infinite compassion before he turned from the fresh-sown grass toward the naked black crosses.

'Come with me,' he said, 'and I will show you where your son lies.'

When Helen left the Cemetery she turned for a last look. In the distance she saw the man bending over his young plants; and she went away, supposing him to be the gardener.

Delivered by Kipling so subtly and tenderly, Helen makes the same mistake as Mary Magdalene going to visit the tomb of her Lord and Teacher on that first Easter morning. For me, this is one of the most moving verses in the Bible:

Jesus said to her, 'Woman why are you weeping? Whom are you looking for?' Supposing him to be the gardener, she said to him, 'Sir, if you have carried him away, tell me where you have laid him, and I will take him away.'

John 20.15

Helen's 'mistake' goes uncorrected; Kipling's story ends. But in John's gospel, 'the gardener' reveals his identity to Mary. And she rushes back to the other disciples with the most extraordinary news you could possibly imagine: 'I have seen the Lord' (John 20.18). John doesn't record their reaction. But Luke tells us her words 'seemed to [the disciples] an idle tale, and they did not believe them' (Luke 24.11). How could she say such a foolish thing at such a moment? Had she completely lost the plot?

Plots proceed according to an accepted and believable order and structure. Plots are habits of thought, traditional, time-honoured conventions. Writing screenplays, I was always terrible at plotting. Plots felt like an imposition somehow. My writing partner and I usually found ourselves being asked to develop dramas based on historical research. We lost ourselves in Edwardian Whitechapel or in the boiler rooms and coal bunkers of *RMS Titanic*; we lived in the Dutch East Indies during the 1880s, under the shadow of a famous volcano; or on the streets of Ancient Rome. We loved the worlds and the characters we encountered there. Squeezing them into plots that had to fit around advert breaks and 'serial arcs' and the whims of witless producers broke my heart in the end.

What I love about parish ministry is its plotlessness. Happily, like Mary, I've lost the plot.

In 1962, Thomas Kuhn published *The Structure of Scientific Revolutions*, in which he argues that science does not proceed or progress in an orderly, plotted fashion. 'Normal science,' he says, 'the activity in which most scientists inevitably spend almost all their time, is predicated on the assumption that the scientific community knows what the world is like.' The assumption 'what the world is like' is open to question (not least, open to question by science), and it is periodically demolished and orthodoxies overturned, resulting in what Kuhn calls a Paradigm Shift. The old models don't work any longer; new models make better sense of the world, are less leaky. What's more, it's our errors, our mistakes, our ignorance, Kuhn argues, that often point us in this new direction.

When Jesus returns briefly to his home town, he finds he 'could do no deed of power there' (Mark 6.5) because the people dismiss him, take offence at him. Isn't this the carpenter? In short, the people of Nazareth don't need to believe in Jesus; they assume they know him. But Jesus' miracles all take place in a context of overturned assumptions, loss and searching. The people he is able to help *need* him; they can't afford to question him or dismiss him. Faith is much closer to needing than to knowing. At first glance this seems to put the religious believer fundamentally at odds with the scientist But actually it draws them closer together. Like scientists, Christians are devoted to pursuing what they don't know. So, St Augustine warns us, 'If you understand it, it's not God'. And Thomas Aquinas follows suit, saying 'To comprehend God is impossible for any created intellect'. And the anonymous author of *The Cloud of Unknowing*, the fourteenth-century masterpiece of British mysticism, urges us to try to overthrow all knowledge and feeling of anything below God, and trample it down deep beneath the cloud of forgetting.

When Mary Magdalene realises she's standing in the presence of the risen Lord Jesus, her desperately moving first impulse is to cling to him. All her assumptions of what the world is like crumble away.

What the story of Mary's encounter with Jesus offers us is a perfect example of how to lose the plot, how to be blessedly mistaken and how to break through the old, hard-won habits of knowing, to needing. By not trying to bend the world to how we think it ought to be plotted, we are able to emerge authentically into our story, living in the unruly reality of a risen, uncontainable love, the gardener's infinite compassion.

Lord, when we fail to recognise you,
call our name.
When we fail to acknowledge you,
call us yours,
And when we fail to follow you,
call us back.

AMEN

. . . . .

I'M STANDING AT THE GATE behind my house, watching Philip, the shepherd, calling the ewes and checking on their new lambs. I watch one lamb uncollapse itself to stand for the first time, shadowed by the bulk of its mother.

Used to people, these sheep are always friendly, inquisitive. Even so, Aggie is wary whenever they come running towards her. I tell her, it's greeting not aggression, but she's not convinced, and cowers. The sheep are interested in us, but they trust Philip, they need him.

Researchers at the University of Cambridge published findings recently that appeared to show sheep are able to identify individual human faces. In laboratory tests, the Cambridge sheep could tell the difference, apparently, between Fiona Bruce, Emma Watson and Barack Obama.

The implication being, I suppose, that the ability to spot celebrities and politicians is a sign of intelligence; confers some evolutionary advantage perhaps. (I actually wonder whether the reverse might be the case.)

Anyway, sheep are cleverer than we thought. Philip wouldn't have needed a university research unit to tell him this.

The sheep in the Cambridge study were able to recognise celebrities; the sheep in the field behind our cottage are able to recognise Philip. Marvellous. But we're in danger of missing the obvious: they recognise each other, and it's through mutual recognition that they belong together and to one another. They only belong to Philip inasmuch as he can exchange them for their monetary value, but that's a thin definition of belonging. If the experience of this pandemic is teaching us anything, perhaps it's our coming to appreciate what 'belonging' really means, what it means truly to belong to one another, to belong in communities and families and flocks. We are learning the value of our belonging, rather than the value of our belongings.

After the resurrection, when Jesus appears to Doubting Thomas, he gives him a singular instruction: 'Do not doubt, but believe' (John 20.27). In English, as in many European languages, the word 'doubt' has the same root as the word 'double'. So, when we doubt, we say we're in two minds. If something is sure and certain then there's no shadow of a doubt. Doubts cast shadows, double themselves, proliferate. Doubts creep in. They're plural and pluralising.

But when Jesus comes and stands among his disciples, he does so after his atoning actions on the Cross. His saving atonement is an at-one-ment. That's what atonement means, a making one. Jesus does the opposite of doubling. Doubts double, faith unifies.

I can't stand apart from others without coming apart myself.

.....

A FRESHNESS HAS GONE FROM THE AIR. The barley is already waist high and wispy. The puddles are muddy craquelure.

Living close to Salisbury Plain, I am used to traces of a military presence all around. I have parishioners, retired from local regiments, who assemble in pews and pubs, polishing their shoes on the backs of their trousers, clicking smartly up the aisle to read the lesson on Sundays. Brave and kind, and often very funny, they look out for one another, offering a taxi service from hospital after cataract ops, picking up prescriptions, or doing each other's shopping.

And in the landscape too, there's often a military aspect: decoy flares, infrared countermeasures, hanging ghostly over the downs at Market Lavington, 'tanks crossing' signs on isolated lanes, occasionally actual tanks crossing, the rumbling of ordnance on summer nights, like a storm that never hits.

But even I was shocked yesterday when a chinook helicopter thundered low over the beech clumps at the top of the hill, shadows of its rotors scything madly at the maize. I stopped in the middle of the rutted path that runs between the fields and *felt* the helicopter pass overhead. Everything shudders.

The ungainly thing tilts slightly and I see up into its body. A soldier hangs in the back, looking out over the open loading ramp. He waves down at me. I wave back.

And he's gone, heading north-west, towards Martinsell and Marlborough, but the wave stays long after the clattering has faded into the afternoon. I sit down on the bank and feel overwhelmed.

What is it about that brief shared moment that moves me? It's that the soldier's waving brought us briefly close, but at the same time emphasised the distance separating us. Like we're in separate worlds.

> My friends and companions stand aloof
>     from my affliction,
> and my neighbours stand far off.

Psalm 38.11

We share so much with the psalmist these days. How long is it since I hugged my friends? Distance and separation and loss are deep stresses on how we experience the world, and a painful alteration in how the world discloses itself to us. We yearn for connection, but real connection, we feel, is impossible at a distance. According to Aristotle, we can lose our sight, or our hearing, our sense of smell and taste, and go on living. But if you can't touch or feel touch, then you're not alive. Almost: I touch therefore I am. *Tango ergo sum.*

Our ingenious attempts to deny the power of distance – printing, telecommunications, social media, Facetime, or just waving – all serve to illustrate how distance is *the* obstacle.

I've heard it said it takes a newborn some time to be able to conceive of itself as separate from the world. For the first few weeks of her life, a baby can't tell where she ends and her mother begins. There is no separation, no distance. We yearn for that state, I think, for the rest of our lives, anxiously, broken off from the whole, isolated, self-isolated even. And yet there's a secret gift in this too. In a posthumously published collection of notes and journal entries, the French philosopher and theologian, Simone Weil (1909–1943), offers this fragment, a perfect parable:

> Two prisoners whose cells adjoin. They communicate with each other by knocking on the wall. The wall is the thing that separates them but is also the means of communication. It is the same with us and God. Every separation is a link.

What divides us, distance, the gap between us, is actually the medium by which we're connected to one another, and to God. Generally we think of all gaps as bad news: gender pay gaps, funding gaps, gaps in our knowledge. Gaps are shortfalls and failings. To the opportunist, there's a gap in the market. Gaps imply something's missing, or something's fallen out: a tooth perhaps, or the three of clubs. Or been forgotten. Or deliberately redacted; gaps can be suspicious, a withholding. Gaps leave us at a loss, and when we grieve, we talk of a gap in our lives. Nonetheless, the last thing we look for when we grieve is 'closure'. I don't find grieving people want to close these gaps in their lives; they know healing isn't in closing, but in remaining open. These gaps, as Simone Weil's parable suggests, are precious, if painful. Our lives are richer for the gaps, the separations. A life without gaps wouldn't be a human life any more than a comb without gaps would be useful to a hairdresser. In fact, all our human arts and sciences depend on the gap. Gaps are life-giving, like lungs, those gaps in the middle of ourselves where life goes in and out. So, when the atheist describes God forced into retreat by the advance of science as a 'God of the gaps', I see the phrase as an accurate description, not a dismissal.

For me, the most moving passage in the Bible, the passage that contains everything that consumes me about the Christian faith, is to do with distance, a gap, and crossing it. A son has left home, spent his time and his inheritance foolishly, selfishly. Desperate and full of regret, he decides to return.

> 'I will get up and go to my father, and I will say to him, "Father, I have sinned against heaven and before you; I am no longer worthy to be called your son; treat me like one of your hired hands." So he set off and went to his father. But while he was still far off, his father saw him and was filled with compassion; he ran and put his arms around him and kissed him.'
>
> Luke 15.18–21

'I will get up and go to my father...' 'When he was still far off... he ran to him.' That mutual yearning – a parent for a child, a child for their parent – is the dynamic of the whole of creation. Creation is personal. And there is a call that runs through all things, across the gap: to connect.

. . . . .

EVERY AUTUMN AND WINTER, the twenty-metre stretch of grass up to my front door becomes a mud slide. At least one of us goes head over heels at some point. So we resort to trudging through the hogweed and tussocky long grass under the apple trees instead. But with bins or shopping or vestments, it's not practical.

So while it's warm and dry, my friend Paul is digging out a proper path using his mini-excavator to strip off a few inches of chalk and flint (there's hardly any topsoil here) in order to lay the foundations for a new brick path.

During the course of the dig, we've unearthed the usual bent nails, a shilling, fragments of mass-produced willow pattern chinaware, the stem of a clay pipe. The fields around here are littered with lead musket balls from the Civil War. If you make an effort to crack them open, the flints are full of fossils. And from a young age, my friend Noah was able to return home after any walk over the downs with a clutch of meteorites: gobs of iron, a giant's knuckles. He could just reach down and pick them out of ploughed fields like potatoes.

The other evening, as I climbed the hill behind my house, I saw a shooting star. Not one of those blink-brief ticks across the sky, but an arcing dissolution, a silent spray of sparks, high in the atmosphere's shallow, upturned bowl.

The feast of the Ascension was over a week ago but I'm still thinking about those touchingly naïve depictions of the disciples looking up into the sky at their departing Lord, his bare feet poking out of the clouds. In looking up at shooting stars, say, or ascending Christs, we're in danger of failing to notice what's under our feet, what's buried, left behind, the remnants.

The Bible is built on a remnant. The Jews who return after Exile in Babylon are referred to as the Remnant. 'But now I will not deal with the remnant of this people as in the former days, says the Lord of hosts' (Zechariah 8.11). And the disciples, the earliest church, those left behind at the Ascension, are themselves a remnant of Christ's ministry. The New Testament tells the story of the birth of a ragged remnant.

Mark's gospel is generally accepted to be the earliest of the three so-called synoptic gospels. And Matthew mines ninety per cent of Mark for use in his own gospel; Luke uses about fifty per cent. So only tiny little bits of Mark remain unique to him, bits ignored and overlooked by later plundering evangelists. To my mind, these passages are like fragments of things left to lie forgotten in the ground, remnants. This is one:

> He also said, 'The kingdom of God is as if someone would scatter seed on the ground, and would sleep and rise night and day, and the seed would sprout and grow, he does not know how. The earth produces of itself, first the stalk, then the head, then the full grain in the head. But when the grain is ripe, at once he goes in with his sickle, because the harvest has come.'
>
> Mark 4.26–29

A whole parable. Not just a disembodied china handle or coinage in a forgotten currency or a musket ball in a world without muskets. Surely this passage is serviceable?

Actually, it's more than serviceable. Nested in this remnant are further remnants, the seeds the farmer leaves in the ground. Remaining there, they grow. He knows not how. Remnants have a habit of taking root, flourishing when we're not looking, not involved. While we can act in the world – sowing, sleeping, rising, reaping – stuff happens regardless, unplotted and unexplained, under our feet.

Last week, slightly reluctantly, we drove our squatter cat back to her owners in the next village. Within a couple of hours, though, she's back, jumping up on the kitchen table where I'm working, and trying to climb on my shoulders, purring in my ear.

The essential property of a remnant: it belongs. Even if separated, it belongs. Handles to cups, stems to pipes. This cat to us, apparently. Aggie adores her.

Now, I've never owned a pet before (unless you count Joey's lizard). An actual cat. So, when it comes to looking after her – I do not know how.

And perhaps that's just as it should be.

.....

TIDES OF SNOWDROPS, crocuses, speedwell and primroses rise and fall over the churchyard. And now cow parsley drifts against the sun-warmed walls. Everything was beginning to wilt and go over in the long cloudless days. But it's fresher this morning, the ground wet with the night's rain, and the blades of wheat in the fields beyond the churchyard are each tipped by a bead of water with a world inside. And I'm wearing a duffel coat.

Out along the tops, the rutted tracks are filled with reflected sky. On my walk this afternoon, as I climb up the banks to avoid puddles, I'm reminded of a poem by Thomas Traherne (1636–1674). Little known in his lifetime, Traherne, clergyman and peculiarly imaginative theologian, is now generally bundled with John Donne, George Herbert and Henry Vaughan as a metaphysical poet. But the label doesn't quite fit. Traherne is more proto-romantic, more mystic than metaphysician. His poem 'Shadows in the Water' is almost science fiction. He imagines himself a child playing by the edge of a puddle.

> Thus did I by the water's brink
> Another world beneath me think;
> And while the lofty spacious skies
> Reversèd there, abused mine eyes,
>     I fancied other feet
>     Came mine to touch or meet;
> As by some puddle I did play
> Another world within it lay.

He populates this puddle, this reflected world, with 'yet unknown friends' and companions, playmates. And yet he knows

> They seemèd others, but are we;
> Our second selves these shadows be.

Sceptical at first, I've been hosting and leading Sunday worship using Zoom for several weeks now. And actually I find it very moving to see familiar and less familiar faces from the parishes and beyond arranged on the screen like a vast game of Celebrity Squares, or those perforated grids of Green Shield stamps my mother used to collect while shopping on the high street in the village where I grew up.

And all the little faces – second selves – calling out to one another and waving. We all feel like Traherne looking into the puddle, seeing our friends:

> Whom, though they were so plainly seen,
> A film kept off that stood between.

While it's the puddle that offers this possibility of contact with our second selves, it is also, as Traherne recognises, that which separates us. Likewise, video conferencing platforms or social media applications claim to be in the business of connecting us all. But we should never forget, they are 'media', films, surfaces: they stand in the middle, between us. Perhaps this explains why, sitting at my desk with hundreds of participants on the screen in front of me, I sometimes feel an overwhelming sense of loneliness.

Our Sunday services on Zoom are like crowds on the surface of my screen. When the crowd expands, it spills over onto another 'page' and then another and another, like a party into different rooms of the same house. It's hard to pick out faces in the crowd, just as it is in real crowds. I think it's this jostling and mixing that makes Zoom services sometimes so moving, and so medieval. Church has become again the space where we meet one another and catch up on neighbourhood news. And in this respect, I'm lucky: medieval ministers didn't have a 'mute all' function with which to quieten their noisy flocks.

Last Sunday, to well over two hundred worshippers on Zoom, Mrs P chose to read the gospel with a budgie perched on her shoulder. Vigorously bobbing up and down, Bertie squeaked and squawked throughout, thoroughly enjoying his few minutes of fame. (Ears pricked, the squatter on my lap began to pay attention to the service for the first time.) While Mrs P soldiered on, apparently oblivious to Bertie's antics, I could see everyone else laughing. Now, Mrs P would never have dared bring Bertie to church; perhaps our second selves are freer, having more fun in their puddle world.

One of Traherne's inspirations was Neoplatonism, a family of philosophical ideas that flourished between the mid-third century and the fifth but which has had a long and fruitful influence in the 'rare breeds' corners of European thought ever since. In the Neoplatonist's universe, all things proceed *from* simpler causes *into* ever more complex effects, and those effects, by yearning to return to their causes, are telescoped back ultimately into the one, simple, Cause of all things. This is the heartbeat, the throb of creation.

Writing in the ninth century from the court of the Frankish king Charles the Bald, an Irish Neoplatonist philosopher called John Scottus Eriugena brilliantly maps these ideas onto Christian doctrine. He writes of the return of all things to God as:

> A congregation (*congregatio*), from the infinite and complex variety of things, to the simplest unity of all things, which is in God and is God; so that God

might be all things, and all things might be God.

On my laptop screen every Sunday morning, I see a congregation. 'Congregation' is a word with which we're all more or less familiar and which we use without thinking. But a congregation is more than a group of people (and budgies); it is a gathering. Coming together as a congregation is a way of stepping into the puddle, of belonging, of finding our way home, unmediated, to our cause:

> Of all the playmates which I knew
> That here I do the image view
> In other selves, what can it mean?
> But that below the purling stream
>   Some unknown joys there be
>   Laid up in store for me;
> To which I shall, when that thin skin
> Is broken, be admitted in.

Our gathering – on screens, in the thin film of puddles – is, as Traherne suggests in this final stanza, just a metaphor for our coming together in a way we can only imagine.

> When the complete comes, the partial will come
> to an end... For now we see in a mirror, dimly,
> but then we will see face to face. Now I know
> only in part; then I will know fully, even as
> I have been fully known.
>
> 1 Corinthians 13.10,12

Congregation is our aiming at completion. Today we

are partial, apart; but we will be together, completed.

No one mentioned my sermon last Sunday. But Bertie the budgerigar is a star. One of the trials of a virtual ministry, I suppose. One, but not the worst. Frankly, I'm longing for parishioners again, rather than 'participants'.

.....

CLICK-CLICK. PAUSE. Click-click-click.

Illicitly, I'm in church saying Morning Prayer. It's the first time I've been inside the building for weeks; air damp, floor crunchy in places with bat droppings. But the summer sun in the stained glass smears and shuffles golds and blues and reds on the walls.

Click-click-click.

What *is* that? Emerging into the light, I see a song thrush on the church wall determinedly tapping a snail against the brick, doing her best to gain entry, to extract the tasty escargoo inside.

Click-click-click.

I can't help feeling sorry for the snail. He's done his best to protect himself from the world, to hide himself inside. He's organically self-isolated. Locked down by nature, opened up by force, a vulnerable, hidden life.

Last summer, I worked for a charity that took a group of British teenagers to The Gambia in West Africa. Our aim was to devise, rehearse and present a performance with young Gambian actors and singers, and our subject – chosen by the teenagers of both countries – was identity. Who are we when we're unhidden, broken open?

When Samuel is sent by God to Bethlehem in order to

anoint a replacement for Saul as king of Israel, the first candidate he is presented with is Eliab, son of Jesse. Surely, it's him, a fine, upstanding young man? But God says:

'Do not look on his appearance or on the height
of his stature, because I have rejected him. For the
Lord sees not as man sees: man looks on the outward
appearance, but the Lord looks on the heart.'

1 Samuel 16.7

God doesn't need to crack the shell in order to see the person inside.

In The Gambia, we used music, tribal dance, song and folk tales to try to see behind the casing of our cultural inheritances and borrowings. The British teenagers told a story from Scotland about a selkie. A selkie resembles a seal, but it can peel off its skin, and underneath it's a beautiful woman, or a handsome man. The story goes like this: coming ashore in a hidden bay one summer's day, a selkie takes off her seal skin and dances on the beach in the sun. A man spies her and wants her, so he steals her seal skin and hides it away.

The man and the selkie woman marry, have children and remain together many years. A devoted mother, the selkie woman is nonetheless sometimes filled with a longing for the sea.

One day, her children find an old trunk. At the bottom of the trunk is a skin, a remnant from her previous life. Not knowing what it is, the children show it to their mother. She immediately recognises her seal skin, takes it to the seashore, pulls it on and disappears into the sea.

The waves close over her silky head.

The selkie made her place in the world, but something – she knows not what or how – calls to her from a gap in her heart. Afraid of the gaps, we're all selkies, hiding ourselves, hiding *from* ourselves; we grow shells.

An Ancient Greek word for person is *prosopon*. It means 'before the face', a mask. In Latin, *persona* literally means 'that through which sound passes'. To both the Greeks and the Romans, a person is a mask, specifically a mask used in the theatre to project a character and a voice on stage. Personhood is performed. And behind the mask there are only other masks, other performances. Or is there a self, an identity which lies hidden under the *dramatis personae*, seen only by God?

In a way, this is exactly what the young people were asking in The Gambia. We explored tribal identities: Mandinka, Fula, Karoninka, Wolof and so on. And the British proved just as tribal, though in different ways: nations, class, background, cultural choice. We asked ourselves difficult questions: are gender roles masks? Do we put masks on each other as well as on ourselves?

We rehearsed through the rainy season; but the rains didn't come. Staging the performance in the middle of the village, we were surrounded by noisy, inquisitive children as we set up. Electricity cables were run from the nearby NGO offices; our lighting was lethal, our sound deafening.

As night began to fall, and the performance started, we were interrupted by traffic, by Friday prayers, by last minute nerves. And then – finally – the weather broke: a torrential, biblical deluge. In less than a minute the street was mud, the lighting fused, and everyone was drenched.

We'd worked so hard, for so long, and for what? Standing in the middle of the street in the rain, I was despondent. My shell had been cracked open: that hard and hard-won shell I'd assumed, of responsibility, training and organisation, my wanting everything to go as planned, as contracted, to be a success. My need to get it right, to deserve praise. As though my identity depended on it.

In the capitalist, industrialised world, we've begun to think of our identities as fragile, threatened. We're concerned by the possibility of identity theft. Our bank details, our National Insurance numbers, our medical records and holiday photographs are all stored online, vulnerable to appropriation or misuse. These are real anxieties. But I don't think we should fall into the trap of calling it 'identity theft' when they're pinched. If someone steals my bank account details, I may lose some money, as the selkie woman lost her seal skin, but have I lost my *identity*? She didn't lose hers. Criminals couldn't steal my identity if they tried. If someone stole my identity, there wouldn't be a me to feel the loss: truly, a victimless crime. If anything is unstealable, my identity is.

Back in the rainstorm, the sound crew set up their stack of amps in the dry porch of the NGO office, and they were blasting out Afrobeats, R&B. Everyone was happy, exhilarated, laughing, joyful, singing and dancing in the rain and the mud. Our deep identity is not stealable. It is not performed, not learned, not lived up to, just lived, and lived in the midst of others living. Thus we become offspring of what happens to us, worthy of the story of which we're a part.

Something clicked.

. . . . .

SITTING IN THE CHURCHYARD AGAIN, watching the thrush at work, there's a flicker, like a momentary drop in the day's signal. And looking up, I catch the scimitar silhouette of a buzzard against the blue.

There are kestrels around here too now, recently introduced, hovering and stooping over the young wheat. The farmer has placed nesting boxes in the hawthorn spinneys that run up to the tops.

I often sit on the downs and watch the hawks soaring high on the thermals or in mid-air scuffles with rooks and ragged jackdaws, swooping low over fields and churchyards. Or I catch sight of them precarious in the dead men's fingers of dying ash trees as I drive along the lanes.

When they drift low overhead I feel noticed. Ignored, but noticed. An awareness passes over the land with a hawk's shadow.

What's it like to *see* like that? To see like a hawk?

The eyes of a hawk are tuned for hunting, I suppose; they're like telescopes, picking objects off the horizon and out of their context. The wider landscape is of no interest. Instead, there's a needle-sharp focus on the next meal. Raptors are the ultimate analysts, filtering out the background in order to pick off their prey. We can learn a lot from hawks, from the way they visually scour the world. Because, contrary to popular opinion, the devil is *not* in the detail; God is. 'Even the hairs of your head are counted' (Luke 12.7). The devil prefers generalisations and grand plans; a bureaucrat, he's ruthlessly systematic, good with acronyms. God, on the other hand, is in the nitty-gritty, not at the podium but at the point of need. God doesn't even try to see the wood for the trees. Because it's each individual tree that counts, and is counted.

> How weighty to me are your thoughts, O God!
>      How vast is the sum of them!
> I try to count them—they are more than the sand.
>
> Psalm 139.17–18

God's thoughts get between your toes.

But unlike hawks, we know that details – grains of sand, a field mouse in the unfurling bracken, a single tear – emerge against an infinite backdrop. Perhaps, it occurs to me, we should try to experience the world in a bifocal way, in the details like hawks preying, but along the horizon too, praying.

Prayer is a way of throwing ourselves onto that horizon. Not plucking items *off* it, but letting ourselves and everything else be embraced *by* it, outnumbered by its capacious oneness.

.....

WHEN MY BROTHER AND I WERE YOUNG, our father used to travel a lot for work. And on his return, he'd always bring us a little present, a memento of where he'd been. One time I remember he had a pocketful of small, sea-polished pebbles he'd picked up from a beach in Donegal. He came to fetch us from school that day; it was the first time we'd seen him for weeks. And as he poured these stones into the nests we made of our hands, we were thrilled: the gloss and chill of them, and Daddy home.

Once I asked my niece what it was she loved about her collection of tiny dolls, and she told me, It's because they're little, so little. I knew what she meant. There's something wonderful about small things. A clutch of robin's eggs in a nest, say, a muddy shilling, or particoloured pebbles clinking in the palms of our hands.

As we walked to the car outside the school, my brother burst into tears. He'd already lost his favourite stone, a green one. We retraced our steps, searched everywhere, scoured the ground like hawks for where it might have fallen. Nothing glinting in the gravel. And being green, the stone would never be found if it had fallen in the grass. We searched and searched. But eventually gave up. My brother was inconsolable.

There are lots of small things in the Bible. Mustard seeds, grains of sand, grains of wheat, pearls all spring immediately to mind. They're planted, counted, paid for, sown and so on. But one little thing gets lost.

> 'Suppose a woman has ten silver coins and loses one. Doesn't she light a lamp, sweep the house and search carefully until she finds it? And when she finds it, she calls her friends and neighbours together and says, "Rejoice with me; I have found my lost coin." In the same way, I tell you, there is rejoicing in the presence of the angels of God over one sinner who repents.'
>
> Luke 15.8–10

Clearly, in this parable the lost coin stands for us, for me. The sinner is lost, then found. Cue angelic rejoicing.

But it's too easy, I think, to read Jesus' parables in this way: to say it's about me. It's telling us we should [insert moral lesson here]. Parables as pretty instructions, little lessons. We tend to read ourselves into the parables, but I think we're actually called to read ourselves *out* of them.

The parable of the lost coin would be meaningless if we didn't recognise, perhaps subconsciously, that the small thing – the coin – is nested in the story in a series of crucial relations and significances. The coin *belongs*. It belongs to the woman, it belongs as one of ten, it belongs in the house, it belongs to a system of monetary exchange, it belongs in the spread of emotions, from despair to joy in the story; it belongs in Jesus' intentions for his parable. It even belongs in the way we're reflecting on Jesus' intentions for his parable. And so on. An infinity of belonging.

In one of her most profound and original revelations of divine love, the fourteenth-century English mystic, Julian of Norwich offers a description of a tiny thing. Size of a hazelnut, and lying in the palm of God's hand, is the whole of God's creation, everything. Julian wonders to herself how such a little thing can possibly stay in being.

> For it seemed to me so small that it might have disintegrated suddenly into nothingness. And I was answered in my understanding, 'It lasts, and always will, because God loves it.'

'I was answered in my understanding,' says Julian. Understanding like this amounts to prayer. It's like listening. Rather than skimming the surface of the story, prayer nests us, like the coin, like Mother Julian's hazelnut, in all the significances that comprise God's creation. In prayer, we *belong*.

Walking back to the car from school, my brother starts smiling through his tears, and opens his hand. The stone had been safe in his little palm all the time.

Everything belongs.

.....

I'M UP EARLY TO LET THE CAT OUT. She jumps up on my pillow every morning at about five-thirty, and starts purring and chewing my hair. Quite a liberty when you think we've only known each other a few weeks.

Dawn over the farmhouse roof, like a papercut, clean and precise; it stings. And, to the sound of birds, the planet tilts into the sun. The sky isn't blue; it blues.

John Lennon's atheistical urging in his song 'Imagine' to abandon the notion of heaven has never bothered me. It might even be a good idea. But his suggestion in the next line that above us there's only sky upsets me deeply. *Only* sky? Did he never actually look up? The sky is an endless wonder, our canopy and our context, a far-off boundary, and as close as our breath.

It was the lack of vapour trails in those clear March afternoons that first alerted many of us to the enormity of the virus's impact. Above us, the sky was suddenly untenanted, uninscribed. Tempting too, wasn't it, to see the emptying sky as a return to nature?

Tempting, but not quite right. The aeroplanes we fly in are amazing, but they're not supernatural. An aeroplane is as natural as a butterfly. The former is artificial, made by humans, the latter isn't. Yet human beings are natural too, of course. So are ice particles, sulphur and the combustion by-products of hydrocarbon fuels: the constituents of a vapour trail. It's all part of nature.

Were an alien to visit Earth, they'd quickly be able to infer that a relatively intelligent species was in residence by the presence, among other things, of vapour trails in the troposphere and Saturday night celebrity dancing shows playing on ultra-high frequency segments of the electro-magnetic spectrum. Both signs of intelligence, neither wholly desirable. But both natural.

This apparently opposing pair: natural *or* human-made has cropped up close to home recently. The Kinwardstone or Kenward Stone is an ancient sarsen lying on a hill just south of the Chute causeway, a mile or two from the village where I live. This stone gave its name to the medie-val administrative district of which we're a part: the Kinwardstone Hundred. These days, the stone itself is almost completely forgotten.

Hoping to find it, Johnny and I climbed to the summit yesterday evening. Round here, the hills frown over their valleys, brows furrowed by lynchets, the terracing of ancient field systems.

On our map, the contours – like the lynchets – converge in tight, looping skeins. It's steep. But the view from the top, even in the rain, with clouds blowing in low and busy, is wonderful. We sat, eating smoked trout sandwiches and drinking cheap Côte du Rhône from chipped enamel cups (more of Brother Johnny's Little Treats), and watching the kites and buzzards making the best of it in the blow.

After a certain amount of tramping, hacking and clearing, we found the stone lying in a cup-shaped depression, just below the summit of the down. The depression, one of several that follow the course of the road, is perhaps the remains of a quarry dug out by the Romans when they were building their road which runs, unusually for them, in a curve, along this ridge of hills, connecting Venta Belgarum with Corinium. That is, Winchester with Cirencester.

The Kinwardstone itself is covered in strange markings: a regular pattern of parallel indentations, like a labyrinth, or the convolutions of a brain, or earthworks in a landscape; it frowns. Also known as the Devil's Waistcoat, the stone has unsurprisingly accrued a portfolio of legends: that it's cursed; that the markings depict human entrails. And when someone tried to drag it away with a team of horses, the horses all simultaneously dropped down dead. Or so the story goes.

But it's the argument concerning what caused the markings that fascinates me. Geologists at the beginning of the twentieth century concluded they were the result of glaciation, and deemed them 'natural'. Writing around the time of the geologists' analysis of the Kinwardstone, the American novelist Willa Cather describes the insignificant furrows of a plough in the vastness of the prairie as being like:

> The feeble scratches on stone left by prehistoric races, so indeterminate that they may, after all, be only the markings of a glacier, and not a record of human strivings.

*Only* a glacier.

Nature is full of regularities, of course. You only have to think of ripples in the sand on a beach, or patterns formed by ice on your windows in winter. (On the *inside* of your windows if you live in an old cottage like ours.) Or the endless iterations of the Fibonacci sequence: a flower's petal, a lazy wave's surrender, our own DNA, the fragments of snail shell on the church wall. Nature keeps regular.

But even if – like the lynchets – the patterns on the Kinwardstone were made by one of our ancestors, they'd still be *natural*. We are part of the pattern as much as glaciers. To think, like the geologists, that our work, our regularities, are somehow outside of nature, or beyond nature, is arrogance of the grandest, blindest sort.

It's the underlying naturalness of Jesus' miracles that makes them so powerful. I know that sounds like an oxymoron: a natural miracle. But bear with me.

Any talk of miracles, and we immediately run up against David Hume (1711–1776). Here he is on the subject:

> A miracle is a violation of the laws of nature; and because firm and unalterable experience has established these laws, the case against a miracle is—just because it is a miracle—as complete as any argument from experience can possibly be imagined to be.

Hume's argument rests on a number of assumptions. One could question, for example, the extent to which experience really is 'firm and unalterable'. And how, you might ask, are we ever to establish its firmness and fixity without recourse to further experience? Hume recognises this circularity when he admits that an argument from experience can never be complete, only ever as complete as possible. Most importantly, though, Hume's argument misses its target. We needn't think of Jesus' miracles as violations or breaches, but as fulfilments. They go *with* the grain of nature, not *against* it. Perhaps there's far more of the miraculous in everyday phenomena than we're conditioned to recognise. Perhaps the distinction itself, between miraculous and natural, is of our own devising and doesn't correspond to any observable or measurable feature of reality.

Look at the miracles in the New Testament more closely; most are responses to absence: they have no wine, they have no food, he has no sight, he has lost his mind, they have lost their daughter.

Jesus returns what has been lost, restoring sight, sustenance, health, life. The miracles take place at an intersection between what we've been given and what we've lost, or can lose. It's a human place, familiar in its precariousness and its griefs. The accounts of Jesus' miracles aren't just about his restoring, but our losing; not just about his power, but our vulnerability. In short, these accounts offer us a picture of human experience that is far from 'firm and unalterable' or law-like. The sign of the miraculous is not his power, but our infirmity, weakness and fragility. We can respond to that fragility with a hardening, something like Lennon's 'only' sky, or we can resort to a grandiose conception of ourselves as being outside or above nature, our experience 'firm and unalterable'. Or we can respond *alterably*, opening ourselves to the risk of being altered, miracled. Perhaps that's the point of the miracle stories: they offer us a definition of faith that involves letting ourselves be altered. In faith, we allow ourselves to be marked, like the stone at my feet or the sky above my head. We're not telling the story; we're part of the story being told.

.....

THE MARKINGS ON THE KINWARDSTONE come to mind next day when I'm halfway through sanding down a table. The surface of the table is, like the stone, marked with patterns. The sun has bleached it in patches. And there are rings from coffee mugs; someone (probably me) has spilled red wine across it once.

Lockdown life, I thought, might allow me time to take the table back to its pristine state. But now I'm not so sure.

The stains and marks and dents tell the table's story, just as the grooves in the Kinwardstone tell a story, or stories. What if someone decided to take the equivalent of a sander to me? I'm covered in 'stains'. That tattoo on my ankle I had done with a girlfriend in a grotty parlour under Kensington Market. A mark on my leg where I cut myself clambering over park railings on bonfire night in order to avoid paying at the gates. Or the old scar on my thumb where my brother cut me, accidentally, with a fish-gutting knife we found on a beach in Brittany. The scar, the tattoo, the gouge to my shin (and the rest I haven't told you about): I wouldn't want to lose any of them. They tell part of my story.

Our bodies are most tender where they've been broken, damaged, scarred. The tenderness is important. These are places on our bodies of which we might be embarrassed or ashamed. And so far, I've only mentioned physical damage; unlike tables, we have invisible wounds too. God claims us, as he claims Jacob at Peniel (Genesis 32.22–32), through our injuries and scars. So, Deleuze asks, 'Where do doctrines come from if not from wounds...?' It's through these thin, tender, secret places that we are called most powerfully.

Jesus said, 'Those who are well have no need of a physician, but those who are sick. I have come to call not the righteous but sinners to repentance' (Luke 5.31–32). Would those of you who have no need of a physician, those of you without scars and hurts and regrets please step forward...

No, I didn't think so. Those priests who withhold Holy Communion from the sinful are Pharisees; we're all sinful, all scarred.

Julian of Norwich recognises, as very few do, the deep relationship between damage, discipleship and loving deity:

> We need to fall. For if we did not fall, we should not know how feeble and how wretched we are in ourselves; nor should we know so fully our maker's marvellous love; for we shall see truly in heaven without end that we have sinned grievously in this life and – in spite of this – we shall see his love for us remains intact, and we were never of any less value in his sight. And through this experience of failure we shall have a great and marvellous knowledge of love in God without end.

Which leaves me with a dilemma. What am I to do with this table? The answer, as so often, lies in a favourite children's book. When the brand-new Velveteen Rabbit wants to know what it means to be 'real', she turns for advice to the wise Skin Horse.

'Real isn't how you are made,' said the Skin Horse. 'It's a thing that happens to you. When a child loves you for a long, long time, not just to play with, but REALLY loves you, then you become Real.'

'Does it hurt?' asked the Rabbit.

'Sometimes,' said the Skin Horse, 'but when you're Real you don't mind being hurt. Generally, by the time you're real, most of your hair has been loved off, and your eyes drop out and you get loose in the joints and very shabby. But these things don't matter at all, because then – you're Real.'

I still have both my eyes, although they're not what they were and I have to wear specs these days. My hair is in retreat; I'm not so much loose in my joints as stiff. And, as Emma never tires of pointing out, I'm hopelessly shabby. A martyr to my toenails, I'm often in need of a physician too. I shan't burden you with the details.

We are not born real; we are *made* real, partly by trying to become worthy of what happens to us, but also by being loved, despite our unworthiness, our failings and flaws. And part of loving and being loved means getting hurt, getting scarred.

The table stays stained.

.....

I'VE BEEN GROWING A BEARD. Since I'm going to be isolated, I thought back in March, why not follow Robinson Crusoe's example and let nature take its course? Nature has taken its bristly course. But recently I've questioned myself: doesn't Crusoe shave at all? Decent British chap that he is, he probably fashions a blade from an oyster shell or some such, and dutifully shaves in a nearby rock pool. So, this week I ordered beard clippers online. Yesterday they arrived. But then I happened on this passage in Augustine's *City of God*:

> There are some details in the body which are there simply for aesthetic reasons, and for no practical purpose – for example the nipples on a man's chest, and the beard on his face.

You can leave my nipples out of it, but the beard? The clippers stay in their box and the beard on my chin, 'for aesthetic reasons'. Augustine's point about the body and its details returns me to the table top and its stains. There's something precious, I think, in this obscure remark of Augustine's and in the way the stains on the table top reminded me of my own scars and damaged places. Perhaps the most important lesson of the pandemic will be to do with our bodies. Not just how vulnerable they are, but how precious. And I don't mean that my body – bearded and scarred – is precious to me, or that yours is to you. But that *your* body is precious to *me*, and vice versa. We crave the physical presence of other people. We miss each other's bodies.

Christianity is often criticised for perpetuating negative attitudes to the body. Its views on sex, sexuality, marriage, birth and so on are often considered superannuated, patriarchal and body-hating. But these criticisms (while far from completely groundless) often rest on questionable assumptions, and are frequently expressed from standpoints that themselves have dubious track records when it comes to attitudes to the body.

Accounts of the body that are critical of a Christian stance are likely to derive from Enlightenment thinking. Descartes (1596–1650) argues that mind and body are two distinct and separable substances, concluding that he is 'a thinking thing' to which a material body is closely conjoined. His body remains independent *of* him and usable *by* him for as long as he lives. Body as more or less compliant helpmeet for the heroic (male) mind. Consciousness has a Crusoe quality: male and marooned in a partially tameable *terra incognita*.

Thomas Aquinas (1225–1274), on the other hand, whose *Summa Theologiae* is a meticulously reasoned compendium of Catholic doctrine, thinks of the human being as a soul-body unity. My soul is the form of my body: it makes me what I am, beard, nipples and all. The form is essentially an arrangement of matter. As the form of the body, the soul is integrated with the body. Our bodies are not joined to us, nor us to them. When I go for my morning walk to the top of the hill behind my house, it's not a case of one substance (my mind or soul) moving another more or less biddable substance (my body); no, it's a case of Colin moving Colin, *one substance* moving itself up the hill.

For Descartes, and those who followed him, the body is an instrument of the soul or mind. For Aquinas, and those in the Christian tradition, the body is an integral part of *who I am*. In this respect, as so often, Nietzsche nails it:

> The body is a great reason, a manifold with one sense, a war and a peace, a herd and a herdsman... There is more reason in your body than in your finest wisdom.

Covid-19, we might be tempted to say, has revealed how vulnerable our bodies are to a tiny subcellular organism. But check the language here. Actually, our bodies are not vulnerable to the virus, *we* are. As a matter of course, as a matter of language, we are all heirs of Descartes, drawing a distinction between our bodies and ourselves. Some scientists and philosophers have tried to convince us we can think and speak in this divorced and possessive way of our bodies. But we don't have bodies; we don't have minds; we are persons. Christian attitudes to the body have often, I think, been more clear-eyed, honest and accepting than those of some of its prudish (and generally bearded) detractors.

Finding our bodies a source of shame and embarrassment is, scripturally speaking, a symptom of sinfulness and disobedience.

> Adam said 'I heard the sound of you in the garden, and I was afraid, because I was naked; and I hid myself.' He said, 'Who told you that you were naked?'
> Genesis 3.10-11

God's point: you have to be *told* you're naked. We're not naked until we're told we're naked in the same way we're innocent until proven guilty.

Someone I know, someone vehemently opposed to the Church and all she believes it represents, recently expressed the view to me that the spread of coronavirus through care homes and among the physically weak is a good thing. It's a case, this person went on, of nature taking its course and carrying off those who shouldn't really be alive anyway. These views have their shallow roots in off-the-peg Enlightenment dogma and pseudo-science; they see the body as a machine, and life as its mechanical functioning. If you need an example of body-hating language, here it is.

For Christians, on the other hand, the occupants of the beds in our care homes and hospitals are not malfunctioning machines, but *people*.

I have a treasured signed copy of a book called *Patients Come First: Nursing at 'The London' between the Two World Wars* by Margaret Broadley. It provided valuable source material when I was researching an historical TV drama series set at the London Hospital. Writing in 1980, Margaret looks back at her life as a nurse in the East End. She ponders what's changed, and what's remained the same, and describes how she and other new nurses 'entered the hospital with "Can I help you?" written on our hearts. One thing that has stood the test of time and remains unchanged is "Can I help you?"'

Margaret and her colleagues, it seems to me, and the exhausted nurses and doctors of our own day, all exemplify a deep truth. What's important about a calling or a vocation – to nursing, say, or to ministry – is not so much who it's *from*, but who it's *for*.

.....

CAN I HELP YOU?

Is that the vicar? Oh, please, Father. I'm in trouble.

Yesterday afternoon I received a phone call from a woman sitting on the steps of St Katharine's. Her words were coming out in a confused tumble; she was on the edge of panic and kept apologising, saying she needed to speak to a priest.

A passer-by came on the line and told me the woman in front of her was soaked from the rain and needed help. I said I'd be there in fifteen minutes.

I jumped in the Ibiza and drove to St Katharine's in the forest. But when I reached the church, I found no one there. I rang the number back and the woman insisted she was sitting outside St Katharine's. I looked about, slightly unnerved now. Not a soul in sight. St Katharine's church in Burbage, she insisted on the other end of the phone. The church in nearby Burbage is All Saints', not St Katharine's. Easy mistake to make, I thought, and got back in the car, heading for Burbage now. The phone rang again. Desperate, she wanted to explain her location exactly. She told me she could see the pub opposite the church. The Cross Keys, she said. I pulled over. The Cross Keys? The nearest Cross Keys pub closed years ago, and it wasn't in Burbage anyway.

And then the penny dropped. Where is Burbage? I ask. Outside Hinkley, she says, off the M69. Leicestershire. I am in Wiltshire. Burbage, near Marlborough. We're hundreds of miles apart.

I stood in the rain, realising there was nothing I could do to help this person whose voice was broken now with sobs. I'm so sorry, I said.

Back at my desk, and after a quick Google search, I rang *St Catherine's*, in Burbage, Hinckley, and left a message, giving them the woman's number. I've no idea if they picked it up. Putting the phone down, I wondered at how I'd assumed I knew where this person was just because the names she used were familiar. An unnoticed muddle, and she and I had believed we were in the same place at the same time. It was almost magical, like a spell cast in a fairy tale, or a curse, a feeling heightened by the fact that St Katharine's (as opposed to St Catherine's) is deep in Savernake Forest.

In medieval Romance literature, knights often find themselves lost and baffled in a forest. In his narrative poem, 'Yvain, The Knight of the Lion', Chrétien de Troyes tells the story of Calogrenant, one of King Arthur's knights, who travels along a path choked by brambles and briars running through the enchanted forest of Brocéliande, where he gets into all sorts of scrapes.

Courtly romance literature, of which Chrétien's poem is a fine example, has a peculiar quality. The emphasis is always on the inner chivalric values of the knight, meaning that the 'real world' becomes more and more fictitious, flimsy and fantastical. The moral dimension of events is their sole reality, and so a series of incidents assumes the status of a quest.

Like medieval knights, Christians live by a code, a set of

values that do not derive from or depend on the world. So, Jesus tells Pilate, 'my kingdom is not from this world' (John 18.36). And Christians are called to set their minds not on things of this world, but on divine things (Mark 8.33), and to live not by the world's law, but by love. God's kingdom, for Christians, is the ultimate reality. And the 'real things of this earth' are partial and passing.

As in a fairy tale or an Arthurian romance, the 'real' world with its names and its ways and its wireless technology can trick us. It can make a damsel in distress appear and disappear in the blink of an eye, and leave us alone in the forest. It can convince us we're close when really we're far apart.

Mobile to my ear, I stood in the rain on the edge of the forest, halfway to Burbage which wasn't Burbage.

> 'The kingdom of God is not coming with things
> that can be observed; nor will they say, "Look, here
> it is!" or "There it is!" For, in fact, the kingdom of
> God is among you.'
>
> Luke 17.20-21

Neither of us here nor there, but somehow in between, we prayed down the line.

Perhaps, when Jesus tells the disciples that the Kingdom of God is among us, it's not meant as reassurance, but challenge, as a quest. And maps and mobiles won't help.

. . . . .

AN AMBULANCE CAME FOR GARY. When they

arrived, paramedics put an oxygen mask over his nose and mouth. They told him to breathe slowly and deeply. Gary nodded, his face half in shadow, eyes frightened; he was looking up at me and Theo.

Over the last few months, we've grown really fond of Gary. Every week, when we're out delivering food around the parish, we always stop for a chat. Generally he's smoking with his mates under the wooden shelter in the gardens of the housing unit where he lives. But sometimes we go upstairs and drop his shopping off outside his flat. He answers the door in his briefs and a singlet and apologises for his state of undress. For reasons known only to himself, Gary refers to his briefs as his 'Iraqis'.

But yesterday we came across Gary collapsed on the forecourt of the local petrol station, slumped in the shade at the foot of the signage mast and fighting for breath. Not in peak physical condition, Gary had been overcome by the heat after pottering down to the garage to buy his daily litre of Cherry Coke and a packet of Lambert and Butlers.

While the ambulance was still on its way, Gary was told not to eat or drink anything. That didn't stop him tucking into a packet of Wotsits. You're not supposed to be doing that, Gary. Gary held up the crisps. Breakfast, he said. 'Most important meal of the day.' There's no arguing with Gary.

Truth be told, Gary's not the easiest of people, and his neighbours have occasionally questioned why we're helping him at all. It's simple enough – too simple – to answer with 'Love your neighbour as yourself'. This is the law delivered to Moses, and St Paul elaborates on it in his letter to the Romans: 'Love does no wrong to neighbour;

therefore, love is the fulfilling of the law' (Romans 13.9–
10). In helping Gary, we're fulfilling the law by which we
choose to live. But that's clearly not an adequate response
to those questioning the wisdom and kindness of our
actions; it fails to answer their question. Is it loving to support someone who thereby feels enabled to maintain a set
of negative behaviours? Forty fags a day and litres of pop.
Rather than supporting Gary, should we not be encouraging him to support himself? Love can be tough; it can be
expressed as 'no'. After all, another of the laws from
Leviticus stipulates, 'You shall reprove your neighbour, or
you will incur guilt yourself' (Leviticus 19.17). Shouldn't
we be reproving Gary, or finding someone more deserving?
Wouldn't that be the loving action? Are we not actually
doing wrong to our neighbours and therefore failing by our
own lights? These are good questions.

And a good answer can't rely on concepts such as duty
or law because we'd then have to assume our dutiful, legal
actions were loving. And it's precisely that assumption that
is in question. Love your neighbour is law, but it doesn't
follow that the law is always loving.

There's another answer, altogether different and more
demanding. I heard it from the mouth of Ken, a wise and
caring parishioner who looks out for Gary. We don't love
Gary, he said, because we're told to as Christians. We don't
love Gary because it's our duty as Christians. We don't love
Gary because it tells us to in the Bible. We love Gary
because, like us, he's made in the image of God.

In 1930, Anders Nygren, a Swedish Lutheran theologian, published *Agape and Eros*. Nygren draws a radical
distinction between two forms of love. *Eros*, he character-

ises, essentially, as the sort of love that might result in our withholding charitable support for Gary in order to 'help' him help himself, or to help someone more 'deserving'. *Eros* love is conditional. It judges worth in the loved object. Nygren describes it as 'acquisitive' because it acquires for itself moral data from the world by means of which it makes judgements. The ego sits near the surface of *eros*'s ethical judgements. Yes, I love; but on *my* terms and according to *your* deserts.

*Agape* love is different, the reverse, in fact. Nygren's starting point, like Ken's, is that we are made in the image of God. God's love must therefore serve as the paradigm for our loving one another. God's love, Nygren says, is limitless, spontaneous and unmotivated. By that, he means God is essentially loving; God cannot *not* be loving. And God is therefore indifferent to value. It's not on account of who we are or what we do that God loves us; it's on account of who God is that we're loved regardless of who we are and what we do. God's love is not bestowed in response to perceived value in us; it's through His loving us that God bestows our value in the first place.

Standing in the shade of the petrol station canopy, I watch Gary being helped into the ambulance by paramedics in full PPE. And as he's driven away down the A338 towards Swindon, I pull on my mask and go into the shop to thank the staff for their attentiveness. While we'd waited for the paramedics, they'd brought Gary cups of water and a baseball cap to keep the sun off.

I consider buying myself a can of Cherry Coke and a packet of Lambert and Butlers in Gary's honour. Reconsider.

These last weeks, our stories converged, as stories do. I

sense Gary's story may not have a happy ending. But whatever happens – *whatever happens* – it's a love story.

God
Almighty,
Heavenly Father
open us to the world,
draw us into the midst of things
turn us to face away from ourselves
and towards the reality of your presence
all around us all the time: the ground of our being

God
the Son
born among us,
humbly dying for us,
give us strength to follow you
the obedience always to serve you,
readiness to live our lives patterned on you,
our Saviour, our Redeemer: the source of our life

God
the Spirit
inspire us, impel us
to live always to your glory
alert to your grace in every encounter
attentive to your will in all our undertakings
awake to your rich providence in all that befalls us
that we might know you and love you: breath of our breath

AMEN

## MUSIC

**TWO BUTTERFLIES — PAGE 15**
Felix Mendelssohn, *Three Motets*, Op.39 No. 1 Veni, Domine, with Westminster Williamson Voices, conducted by James Jordan on *Hole in the Sky* (Naxos, 2016)

**SITTING ON THE CHURCHYARD WALL — PAGE 15**
Johann Strauss, 'The Radetzky March', played by the Band of the Coldstream Guards conducted by Lt. Col. Douglas Pope, *Military Marches* (Beulah, 2019)

'He's Got the Whole World in His Hands', Mahalia Jackson, vocalist, traditional, *Gospels, Spirituals and Hymns* (Columbia, 1956)

**THE ROOM WHERE I'M WRITING — PAGE 19**
'Morning Prayer', Pharoah Sanders, *Thembi* (Impulse!, 1971)

**HOW FAR CAN I WALK — PAGE 22**
'Big Rock Candy Mountain', arranged and performed by Van Dyke Parks, traditional, on Various Artists, *O Brother, Where Art Thou? Music from the Original Motion Picture* (Lost Highway/Mercury, 2000)

**AT ORDINATION — PAGE 24**
'His Blessings', McCoy Tyner, *Extensions* (Blue Note, 1973)

**AFTER A FORTNIGHT IN BED — PAGE 28**
'Astringent Mouse Trap', Fred Pallem, Le Sacre du Tympan, *L'Odyssée* (Ghost Train/The Other Cast, 2018)

**IT'S WALKING SEASON — PAGE 32**
'The Meadows Go', Ivor Cutler, *Velvet Donkey* (Virgin, 1975)

**AT THE END OF THE FIRST WORLD WAR — PAGE 36**
'Blessed Easter', Holger Czukay, *Rome Remains Rome* (Virgin, 1987)

**I'M STANDING AT THE GATE — PAGE 40**
'Black Sheep Boy', Tim Hardin, *Tim Hardin 2* (Verve, 1967)

A FRESHNESS HAS GONE FROM THE AIR — PAGE 42
'Lord Can You Hear Me', Spacemen 3, *Playing with Fire* (Fire, 1989)

EVERY AUTUMN AND WINTER — PAGE 46
'Piano Piece', Faust, *Faust IV* (Virgin, 1973)

TIDES OF SNOWDROPS — PAGE 48
'I'll be your Mirror', The Velvet Underground, *The Velvet Underground & Nico* (Verve, 1967)

CLICK-CLICK. PAUSE — PAGE 53
'The Sea Calls Me Home', Julia Holter, *Have You In My Wilderness* (Domino, 2015)

SITTING IN THE CHURCHYARD AGAIN — PAGE 57
'Earth Seen from Above', Meredith Monk, San Francisco Symphony Chorus, *Voices 1900-2000: a Choral Journey through the Twentieth Century* (Delos, 2005)

WHEN MY BROTHER AND I WERE YOUNG — PAGE 58
'Boy About 10', Harold Budd, *By the Dawn's Early Light* (All Saints Records, 1991)

I'M UP EARLY TO LET THE CAT OUT — PAGE 61
'Miracle of Love', Swans, *White Light From the Mouth of Infinity* (Young God, 1991)

THE MARKINGS ON THE KINWARDSTONE — PAGE 66
'Tenderness', Sun Ra Trio, *God is More Than Love Can Ever Be* (Saturn, 1979)

I'VE BEEN GROWING A BEARD — PAGE 69
'Solomon's Song', C.O.B (Clive's Original Band), *Moyshe McStiff and the Tartan Lancers of the Sacred Heart* (Polydor, 1972)

CAN I HELP YOU? — PAGE 73
'A Forest', The Cure, *Seventeen Seconds* (Fiction, 1980)

AN AMBULANCE CAME FOR GARY — PAGE 75
'True Love Will Find You In The End', Daniel Johnston, *1990* (Shimmy Disc, 1990)

# SUMMER

I am like an owl of the wilderness,
   like a little owl of the waste places.
I lie awake;
   I am like a lonely bird on the housetop.

Psalm 102.6–7

LYING IN BED WITH THE WINDOWS OPEN, I begin to drift off to sleep. A male tawny owl calls in the trees from the woods behind my house, and a hollowness follows me into my dreams. When I wake in the middle of the night, my head is churning with anxieties.

For a time, it's impossible to tell what's dream and what's not. Did I really open that cupboard on a seething wasps' nest? Did I rummage through all those programmes and publicity from old theatre projects?

The owl and the shreds of dream leave me loosened from reality, adrift, and I wake early, unrested. It's already hot and, after feeding the squatter, I decide to say Morning Prayer in the cool of St Michael's.

Some years ago, I was taught by a wise churchwarden that it's a good idea to leave open church doors in hot weather. The circulating warm breeze takes any damp edge off the air inside, and dries out the old stones and plaster. All very well, but when the protective wire netting over the door frame is as holey and ragged as it is at St Michael's, it means, as today, you may have to share Morning Prayer with an unexpected congregant. A pigeon flaps around in the rafters. Lucky the cat didn't follow me this morning.

When I take a seat in the chancel, the pigeon soon settles and perches on a metal rail above the altar, looking all the while warily down at me. I choose to read the psalms and scriptures out loud today, for her benefit. And she seems to appreciate my efforts.

It's the day in the Church calendar on which we remember the Virgin Mary's visit to her cousin Elizabeth: the Visitation. Both women are with child, Mary with Jesus, and Elizabeth, a few months further gone, with John the Baptist. It's one of the most intimate and moving stories in the Bible. These two pregnant women in a hilltop town of Roman-occupied Judea are the cosmic hinge on which the world turns. And they know it in their bodies. 'When Elizabeth heard Mary's greeting, the child leaped in her womb' (Luke 1.41).

Among all the mosaics decorating the sixth-century basilica of St Euphrasius in Istria is a depiction of this scene. The basilica stands on the shores of the Adriatic at Poreč, ancient Parenzo. This town and its environs must be one of the very few places on the planet where you could've lived your life in four different countries without ever moving house. Until 1918, it was part of the Austro-Hungarian Empire. Then it was in Italy, then Yugoslavia. And since 1991, it has been Croatian. A distillation of European-ness, its narrow streets, wide harbour front and busy markets bear witness to the tidal back and forth of history. On All Souls' Day a few years ago, when I was visiting family there, the autumn breeze in the town was scented with all the chrysanthemums being sold in car parks, on street corners and outside churches, for people to adorn the graves of their loved ones; and that night, high up on the hillsides, the cemeteries were full of flowers and flickering candles.

Taking considerable liberty with Luke's words, the artist who decorated the town's basilica with mosaics chose to include an entirely non-scriptural character in the Visitation panel: a girl holding aside a curtain or veil in order to eavesdrop on the older women's conversation.

It's a brilliant device. The girl's spying presence allows us into the scene. With her, we can listen in on the intensely private conversation. She serves to emphasise the intimacy of the moment. But she also alerts us to the underlying miracle. The portrayal of shock on her face is touching, almost comic: she holds a finger to her open mouth, recognising in a flash that this apparently mundane meeting between two pregnant women is the key to her salvation. To the salvation of the world.

The girl in the mosaic reminds me of that moment in *The Wizard of Oz* when Dorothy finally reaches the throne room of the kingdom. The grand, overpowering architecture, the throne itself, clouds of coloured smoke, all designed to overwhelm: a church, basically. And the Wizard's deep voice booms out, asking who they think they are, daring to come into his presence. Dorothy and her friends quake with fear. The cowardly lion declares he wants to go home.

But then Dorothy pulls aside a curtain to discover the real Wizard, a man of modest appearance and unimpressive mien: a man with a microphone. She and her friends are indignant. It's all a trick, a fraud. This Wizard is just 'a humbug', says Dorothy.

But this humbug has been able to show the Tin man, the Lion, the Scarecrow and Dorothy that what they had needed for their quest, what they were searching for all this time – brains, heart, courage, maturity – deep down they'd had all along. He allows them to see they've become worthy of all that's happened to them.

The reality of this kind man, this humbug, is infinitely more powerful than any smoke-and-mirrors effects. And like Dorothy in *The Wizard of Oz*, that girl in the sixth-century mosaic pulls aside the curtain to reveal for us the truth. Not a king who is terrifying, who demands our humble obeisance, whose promises, like the Wizard's, are always delayed till tomorrow. But a baby in a womb, a king who humbles himself so as to live with us and die for us. A king who doesn't guard his glory but lets it shine on the undeserving. A king who, when he comes, transforms, reveals and redeems without the trappings of worldly power and might.

And whose kingdom is a fantasy.

A fantasy because in a real kingdom, a king lives in a white palace under guard. He makes laws and pronounce-ments, issues orders. Those who don't like the king are kettled and cleared from the streets with tear gas and batons. The king stands in the middle of his city, sur-rounded by his troops and raises a holy book which he takes to be a symbol of power and authority. *His* power and authority. This, more or less, is what a real kingdom looks like.

It doesn't look like a mustard seed (Mark 4.30–32), or

yeast (Luke 13.20–21), or a pearl merchant (Matthew 13.45–46) or a fishing net (Matthew 13.47). We shouldn't underestimate the extent to which Jesus sees his parables of the kingdom *as funny*, a ludicrous pulling aside of the curtain. His disciples knew all too well the Trumpian definition of 'kingdom'; they had Herod, after all, and Rome. To hear of a kingdom that's neither here nor there, or that's like a seed, or yeast or a fishing net is fantastical, and funny.

But if I say the kingdom of God is a joke or a fantasy, do I mean it's like Oz or Narnia or Middle Earth? Precisely not. Fantasy is a vital part of how we come to understand reality, how we come to terms with it (or how we refuse those terms) and how we recognise the call to change it.

Stanley Cavell (1926–2018), one of the most appealing of contemporary thinkers, a champion of what's called Ordinary Language Philosophy, peppered his work with references to the fiction and films he enjoyed. He has this to say about fantasy:

> It is a poor idea of fantasy which takes it to be a world apart from reality, a world clearly showing its unreality. Fantasy is precisely what reality can be confused with. It is through fantasy that our conviction of the worth of reality is established; to forgo our fantasies would be to forgo our touch with the world.

To say the kingdom of God is a fantasy is absolutely not to say it's a fiction, or somehow unreal. Quite the reverse. It's to say, instead, that it requires us rigorously and prophetically to engage our imagination, to hold the reality of our world with its tear gas and tyrants, its smoke and mirrors up to scrutiny, to pull aside the curtain and say, 'Look!'

We want more and more to confuse the kingdom of God with this world. Until there's no discernible difference, and the confusion is complete.

Above all, Jesus' parables of the kingdom are calls to *imagine*. What is tiny now will be vast, capacious; what is mixed invisibly through us will rise around us and lift us; what was hidden will be revealed; what appears to be silly or inconsequential is the source of grace and truth. What this kingdom is will require us to reimagine our world entirely, from scratch. The kingdom of God is an overturning; it's not just another world: it is this world's *other*.

As calls on us to imagine, Jesus' parables are visionary, and radical. And they are anathema to the king in his palace who can call out his troops, enact his laws, press his buttons; but who can imagine nothing. He is executive but he cannot afford to be imaginative. And he cannot afford for you to be imaginative either. So, imagine.

Jesus' kingdom of God is a fantasy in the truest, deepest sense: a powerfully subversive call, an urgent invitation to turn away from a trick and towards the truth. If it sounds like a joke – ask yourself why.

Back in Poreč, in the hemispherical half-dome of the basilica's apse is another mosaic, this one depicting sainted bishops and martyrs approaching a throne against a backdrop of shimmering gold. It's as awesome as Oz's throne room, awesomer. But seated on the throne in majesty is not a mighty king, but a mother and child. Never forget how radical that image is. And above their heads, the Holy Spirit, in the form of a dove.

Above the altar in St Michael's the pigeon watches me, head tilting inquisitively this way and that. Unlike her holy mosaic counterpart, this pigeon makes an unholy mess.

The mop and bucket are in the vestry, behind a curtain.

.....

MERVYN suffers from asbestosis. Breathing is a battle. Yet he takes daily exercise by walking up to the church. As well as coping with his own poor health, Mervyn cares for his wife, who is bedbound. We had a chat this morning, Mervyn and I, in the sunshine. It's hot and Mervyn's wearing his 'Brexit Means Brexit' T-shirt, and shorts. When I ask after his wife, he tells me, 'We've been married fifty-five years'. He pauses. 'I love her,' he says. 'Honestly, I don't know how I'd go on living without her.'

Neither of us speaks for some time, the blessing of Mervyn's words hanging in the two metres of air between us. I think of Emma at home. She still has pains in her chest and she tires easily. But she's recovering, and I thank God.

Mervyn's love for his wife is unconditional; it doesn't depend on anything, certainly not on her health; she no longer recognises him. Rather, his life depends on their love. He lives in love, and 'Those who live in love live in God and God lives in them' (1 John 4.16). In love. Love is not something we can stand outside of, have knowledge of, have a view on. It's the trap we're *in*, the story we're part of. Contrary to what reality TV development teams would have us believe, love is not an island. It's the sea that surrounds the island, the sea that makes the island an island. Love is what makes us us.

Mervyn said his life depended on the love he shared with his wife. That's what it is to be in love. It is to be dependent, but in a wholly life-giving way. Writing in the fourth century, Gregory of Nyssa offers the following gloss on 1 John 4:16:

> Everything that exists depends on Him who is, and nothing can exist except in the bosom of Him who is … Everything that exists is in God, and God is in everything.

When All Saints' is open for Sunday worship, Mervyn often attends. He sits in a pew at the back and struggles to regain his breath after walking up from his bungalow. I don't start the service until Mervyn gives me the nod.

I've been asthmatic since infancy. In a small way, I know how it feels to have to fight for breath. But if I'm honest, at points, asthma has been more of a blessing than a curse: at school, for example, I could spend afternoons happily 'off games' sitting in a warm library rather than running around pointlessly in the cold and mud.

Being asthmatic is a blessing in a more profound way; it serves as a periodic reminder not of my mortality, but the opposite: my vitality. It forces me to recognise that my life depends absolutely and wonderfully on all sorts of prevailing conditions. In this case, of course, on air. On air and my continuing capacity to breathe it.

Under normal circumstances, we take breathing for granted. We take it for granted in church or synagogue or mosque or temple too, failing to notice how much of our worship, whether we're together or alone, depends on puff. In the Vedic tradition (roughly the Indo-Aryan thought-world that would become known to Europeans as Hinduism), the Ātman is the self, the spirit, the imperishable essence. But its root meaning is simply 'breath'. Likewise, in Greek, the spirit is *pneuma*. Or breath. (It's from *pneuma* that English words such as 'pneumatic' and 'pneumonia' are derived.) 'God is spirit,' Jesus tells the Samaritan woman at the well, and *pneuma* is the word he uses in the Greek. 'And those who worship Him must worship Him in spirit (*en pneumati*) and in truth' (John 4.24). *Anima*, in Latin, is the word for soul. But also for breath.

Wherever you're from, breath is holy. Mantras in Buddhism are sometimes characterised as breathing meditations. I've seen it suggested that the Tetragrammaton – *YHWH* – the sign for the unnameable God in the Hebrew Bible, can be thought of as an in-breath and an out-breath: Yah… Weh. Every time we breathe we say the secret name of God. God was hiding right under our noses all along. Every breath a prayer. And those gaps in ourselves, our lungs, are voids for prayer.

Thomas Aquinas defines a human being as a *capax dei*. A capacity for God. To be fully human, we need to embrace and develop within ourselves a lung-like emptiness, a capcity, a void to be filled. Too often we do our best to fill the void with learning, with worldly wisdom, with status. And when we do that, we undisciple ourselves, even unmake ourselves. We feel we can't breathe.

We often talk about faith as something people have or

don't have. But faith itself is actually more of a 'not having'. Our emptiness, our brokenness, our need, our *capacity* – is precisely where the Holy Spirit enters.

God breathes into Adam's nostrils the breath of life (Genesis 2.7). The same God commands Ezekiel to give life to the valley of dry bones in these words:

> 'Prophesy to the breath, prophesy, mortal, and say to the breath: "Thus says the Lord God: Come from the four winds, O breath, and breathe upon these slain, that they may live."' I prophesied as he commanded me, and the breath came into them, and they lived, and stood on their feet, a vast multitude.
>
> Ezekiel 37.9–10

Reminding ourselves of our breath, as Mervyn is reminded all the time, and as the hill behind my house reminds me, is to recognise we live in a state of total dependence. It is to be reminded that our life is gifted to us. I think it's this that Paul is suggesting when he describes God to the Athenians as 'Him in whom we live and move and have our being' (Acts 17.28). He's not actually talking about the sort of God we worship; he's talking about the sort of creatures we are: creatures entirely dependent on the medium in which we exist. Love.

.....

TURN THE IGNITION and you get a sort of dry ticking, an insect-like sound. Nothing more. My car is covered in a thick layer of dust, spattered with bird mess, and the tyres need pumping. One maroon-ish Seat Ibiza looking very sorry for itself indeed. There's moss growing all along the rubber window seals; a spider has taken up residence behind the rearview; and some sort of fungus is beginning to appear in the passenger foot well. The Ibiza is less a car and more a habitat, its own ecosystem. When people talk about 'going green', I don't think they mean it this literally.

I borrow Johnny's jump leads. Clipping the claws to the battery terminals, I feel I'm jump-starting an old life. Not my car's, my own. A life of mileage, diary appointments, meetings, agendas, deadlines. And I was locked down before? I feel I can't breathe.

St Moluag (sometimes known as Lugidus or Lugaidh or Lua) was a Scottish missionary of the sixth century, living around the time the basilica in Poreč was being built on the shore of the Adriatic. Moluag was the founder and abbot of the monastery at Clonfert in County Galway. Bernard of Clairvaux (1090–1153) credits Moluag with the founding of over a hundred monastic houses in Ireland. A busy man then, and well travelled. Yet, for Moluag, the religious life is rooted, static and still. *Ubi stabilitas, ibi religio*, he wrote. 'Where there is stability, there is religion.'

My Seat Ibiza is pure *stabilitas*. It's not going anywhere, even after the application of jump leads apparently.

A contemporary of Moluag, St Benedict (d.547) codified this notion of stability into his *Rule*, the regulations he developed for the religious community he founded at Monte Cassino. Benedict believed, 'Everything necessary... should be inside the walls of the monastery, so that the monks do not need to go wandering outside, for that is not good for their souls.' *Stabilitas*, or staying put, obediently, in the place where you have made your profession, is one of the three obligations of Benedict's *Rule*.

I can proudly say my Seat is the ideal Benedictine car, no chance of it wandering anywhere.

But surely instability, being thrust beyond the walls of the monastery, beyond the comfortable and familiar, lies at the heart of Christian witness from its very beginning? Immediately following his baptism, Jesus is driven by the Spirit out into the wilderness (Mark 1.12; Matthew 4.1; Luke 4.1). And in his turn, Jesus sends the apostles out into a hostile world, instructing them to 'take nothing for their journey, except a mere staff – no bread, no bag, no money in their belt' (Mark 6.7–8). Jesus' own ministry is characterised by movement, by an almost frenzied to-ing and fro-ing, the perpetual push and pull of popular ministry. No *stabilitas* here, no monastery walls.

Better have another go with those jump leads.

Juxtaposing Jesus' life and ministry with Moluag's call for *stabilitas* and Benedict's warnings against venturing outside the walls appears to reveal a genuine and deep tension in the way religious life is lived, or is meant to be lived. Is it ideally static, stable and rooted, or ought it be dynamic, risky, questing, out in the world? While this may appear to be a slightly musty church question, it has a very specific application to our lives now.

From one perspective, our lives during the Covid-19 crisis have been much more Benedictine. There is stability of sorts; we've stayed put. Our way of life has become religious in the original sense. Until recently, 'to be religious' did not mean having faith as a personal or private conviction; it meant being a member of a closed religious order, like the Benedictines, having taken strict vows. Our word 'religion' comes from the Latin *religo, religere*: to bind, to fasten. Religion is lockdown.

But on the other hand, the experience of lockdown has offered us ways of 'wandering outside the walls' that Benedict could not have begun to imagine. We wander the world via Zoom and YouTube and Facebook. The Zoom services I lead on Sundays quickly broke parish boundaries. People log in from all over the world. Viewed in this way, church life is suddenly, radically apostolic again, unmoored from place, moving freely in space, with no money in its belt (as the archdeacon is constantly reminding me).

And in our communities too, walls have broken down. We've recognised afresh the foundational precept of our faith: love one another. So, in the parishes where I work, we've come up with new ways of caring, of being a community, a church. And any historic divide between church and community is being effaced.

The truth is, the stability Moluag and Benedict talk about is not being locked down but opened up. Opened into the world. Freedom and stability are ultimately the same thing. 'If the Son makes you free, you will be free indeed' (John 8.36).

Coughing and spluttering, the engine starts. Clouds of black smoke from the exhaust drift into Godfrey and Mary's garden next door. After all the disparaging, defamatory things I've said about the Ibiza, I'm sorry. We're on the road again, whether that's good for our souls or not.

. . . . .

IN ITS BATTERED STATE, I like to think my rusty Rocinante could've landed a supporting role in a *Mad Max* movie or a political thriller as a shot-up Taliban staff car weaving through the backstreets of Kabul.

But it's a vicar's car. So, following its jump-start earlier this morning, and a first tentative drive to a petrol station, I decide to fork out for a car wash. The platinum option leaves it pretty clean, but here and there stiff saucers of bird shit still remain glued to the paintwork. What do these pigeons eat? It was probably that pigeon from Morning Prayer the other day, I think. And this is revenge for my reading the psalms. I'll need that mop and bucket again.

Back at home, Aggie and I snap on Marigolds and tackle the mess with soapy hot water and an old CD case as a scraper.

A busy half-hour later, and the car looks perfect. Well, as perfect as an '04 Seat Ibiza can ever look. I need the car to be presentable because I've a face-to-face meeting with the bishop tomorrow morning, and my car will be parked on his drive.

One evening a couple of years ago, I was walking through Salisbury Cathedral Close with Bishop Nicholas when he pointed out a particularly filthy car, its registration plate almost completely obscured by mud. 'Look at the state of that,' he said.

'Terrible,' I replied, keys to the offending vehicle – one maroon Seat Ibiza – already in my hand.

Cleaning my car feels like a sort of grubby baptism, marking our emergence into normal life and routine, a preparation for something. For movement perhaps. I feel

I've been still for so long. When God comes to Abraham sitting outside his tent in the heat of the day (Genesis 18.1), he demands movement. From that point on, Abraham is all verb; he runs, bows, brings, hastens. Perhaps that's the key in which all the Abrahamic faiths are written: movement. The children of Abraham are impelled to move, to be changed. In the beginning was the verb.

As God points out to Abraham (Genesis 15.13–14), his descendants will find themselves enslaved in Egypt where they'll encounter a different form of religion, one that remains rigidly static and unchanging century after century after century, what Hegel would call a 'stationary' civilisation. In the first volume of his *History of Religious Ideas*, Mircea Eliade (1907–1986), the influential Romanian historian of religions, discusses the remarkable 'immobilism' of Egyptian religion. He says, 'After the Fifth Dynasty (2500–2300 BC) almost nothing of importance was added to the cultural patrimony', and he goes on to claim that this extraordinary stability is 'the logical consequence of a theology that considered cosmic order to be the supremely divine work and saw in all change the danger of a regression to chaos and hence the triumph of demonic forces'.

Imagine how the God of Abraham, Jacob and Moses must have seemed to the fearful Egyptians. The God of the Israelites is endlessly dynamic, demanding, capricious even, and personal. He enters into a covenant with his people. He has plans for them: 'For surely I know the plans I have for you, says the Lord, plans for your welfare and not for harm, to give you a future with hope' (Jeremiah 28.11).

We all have a tendency towards the Ancient Egyptian, towards the stationary. We create rigid structures for ourselves; we look to the past for patterns and paradigms. We live by habits and hand-me-down customs. We share the fear of the Ancient Egyptians: change is chaos. Isn't it?

Yet, as we've seen in the person of Abraham himself, movement and change is at the very heart of an Abrahamic outlook: repentance is change.

Constructed out of fear, pyramids and presidential palaces are made of stone, arrogant approximations of changelessness. Perhaps a faithful and reasonable approach to a changeless God can only be made through change, through running, bowing, offering, hastening. Cleaning.

'Good morning, Bishop.'

'Hello, Colin. My word, is that a new car?'

. . . . .

PLAGUED BY A HARE that was ruining his crop, a farmer went out and shot it. He failed to kill it, though, and the hare managed to limp away. The farmer followed the mortally wounded animal, and its trail of blood led him to a poor widow's cottage. Inside, he found the widow bleeding out all over the stone flags, from a gunshot wound in her leg. It's a tale from the village where I live.

Down to the tiniest detail I can remember the first time I was scared by a film. My brother and I were little. It was teatime, and we were watching an old black-and-white werewolf movie. It could have been *The Wolf Man* starring Lon Chaney from 1941. I remember clouds thinning and parting to reveal a full moon. The film cuts to a close-up of a man's face, his eyes staring but somehow focussed inwards, as though he's aware of some inescapable and internal tug. He grimaces. Hair begins to sprout, ears to extend. He looks down at his hand as it bristles with new coarse hair, and claws grow from his fingers.

The effects were crude by 1980s standards. My brother and I were growing up on a diet of *Scooby-Doo*, *Dr Who* and Spielberg. But there was something that terrified us in the film. The werewolf wasn't scary. It wasn't the end result – a hairy bloke – that frightened us ; it was the process itself, an unwanted changing from one thing to another.

In her book *Purity and Danger*, the British anthropologist Mary Douglas (1921–2007) argues that fear of change lies behind the Jewish dietary laws. These laws, she says, aim at wholeness and integrity and abominate mixture as contamination. Thus, it is forbidden to plough a field with a donkey and ox yoked together (Deuteronomy 22.9), or for a garment to be made from both wool and linen (Deuteronomy 22.11). It's the blending that is abominable: wolf-man, hare-woman. Obeying the rules is a way of policing the border against mutation, against change. The Israelites inherited something from their years in Egypt. Among the spoils and plunder (Exodus 12.36) is this fear of change, this tendency to the rigid, the pure and the lawful.

When God visits Abraham and Sarah, Abraham is – as we've seen – all action, duty and business. Sarah responds to the change God brings in an entirely different way. She laughs.

> They said to him, 'Where is your wife Sarah?' And he said, 'There, in the tent.' Then one said, 'I will surely

return to you in due season, and your wife Sarah shall have a son.' And Sarah was listening at the tent entrance behind him. Now Abraham and Sarah were old, advanced in age; it had ceased to be with Sarah after the manner of women. So Sarah laughed to herself, saying, 'After I have grown old, and my husband is old, shall I have pleasure?' The Lord said to Abraham, 'Why did Sarah laugh, and say, "Shall I indeed bear a child, now that I am old?" Is anything too wonderful for the Lord? At the set time I will return to you, in due season, and Sarah shall have a son.' But Sarah denied, saying, 'I did not laugh'; for she was afraid. He said, 'Oh yes, you did laugh.'

Genesis 18.9–15

Sarah's secret laugh is one of the great human moments in all scripture. It's a laugh that comes out of change. Her body has changed, as bodies do; it would no longer be possible for her to conceive a child. Her laugh might well be a laugh of bitterness and regret. God is too late, she thinks. God is behind the curve of change. But God *is* the curve of change.

And Sarah's laugh echoes through the whole Bible. In the Greek translation of this passage, the translation with which the gospel writers would have been familiar, Sarah's reason for denying her laugh is given as *ephobethe gar*, for she was afraid. Right at the very end of Mark's gospel, when Mary Magdalene and the other women run away from the empty tomb, they do so *ephobounto gar*, for they were afraid.

My brother and I ran upstairs to our mother, for we

were afraid. We are frightened of only one thing: change. A changeless world would be a fearless world. But it would also be a perfectly dead 'Egyptian' world. Fear is life, and the beginning of wisdom (Proverbs 9.10).

Be afraid.

.....

A NEW AGGRESSIVE FRONT to the light presses shade into retreat under the trees, along walls, to skulk, with the cat, in the lee of things. Even the clouds seem to hang back at the horizon, cowed.

In order to escape the heat, I venture up the hill where the air is fresher. From the top there's a view across the valleys through which the upper reaches of the River Kennet flow. The Kennet rises at Swallowhead Spring, near Silbury Hill, fifteen miles west of here, and joins the Thames at Sonning, a long way east.

Closer still is the River Dun, a tributary of the Kennet. On hot days, local children migrate to the 'dog hole', a shallow pool in the Dun next to the canal and the railway line. In summer, the rivers are full of little crayfish which I've occasionally trapped in a mesh-lined supermarket trolley, and fried with chilli and garlic. Quite tasty. Quite. More crunchy than tasty, to be honest.

At the end of the eighteenth century, the tiny Shalbourne Stream was diverted to feed the newly constructed Kennet and Avon Canal. In 2000, the Shalbourne was returned to its original course through the marshes, debouching into the Kennet at Hungerford.

From where I'm sitting, the downs above Shalbourne are

steep and wooded. But on one shoulder there stands a single tree all on its own. Since March, this tree has taken on a new significance in our house. Aggie calls it the Lonely Tree. She and her friend, Anwen, who lives in the village of Shalbourne, have worked out they can both see this tree from where they live. When lockdown was at its strictest, the girls would communicate on social media using the image of the tree as shorthand for: I'm missing you, I'm thinking of you.

On the wall of the village school is a collage frieze made by the children. At the centre of the frieze, high on a green baize hill, is the lonely tree, a symbol of their rootedness in this beautiful place, a way of saying 'I belong'.

There's a breeze up here today, the air scented with crushed chamomile from underfoot as I climb. And the hedgerows are full of wild geraniums, timothy, poppies, cornflowers and dog daisies. From the top, the fields below have a wan, camouflage quality, patched brown and gold and shades of faded green.

Listen! A sower went out to sow...

When Jesus tells the parable of the sower, it is to a large audience. However, it is only to his disciples that he explains its meaning. He says, 'To you it has been given to know the secrets of the kingdom of heaven, but to them it has not been given' (Matthew 13.11). Access to the kingdom of heaven is conditional. What's more, the conditions appear not to relate to faith or hope or love, but to *knowledge*.

This is unfamiliar territory. In contemporary expressions

of Christianity, we're much more likely to find stress placed on belief, faith, humility, mercy, praise, on loving God and neighbour and so on. There's actually not a great deal to *know*. Is there?

Brother Lawrence warns us, 'We must know before we can love.' And to the medieval mind the idea that religious faith was unrelated to knowledge would have seemed very odd indeed. Back in the thirteenth and fourteenth centuries, entering the university of Paris or Bologna or Oxford to study theology, you would have embarked first on a training which included astronomy, geometry, mathematics and logic. Theology, the longest and most arduous of the courses, was the queen of *sciences*. Theology was knowing stuff.

Writing in the eighth century, the emperor Charlemagne (through his proto-Minister for Education, Alcuin of York) instigates an empire-wide learning programme. The emperor has been worried by the standard of some of the letters he's been receiving from monasteries and bishops in his provinces.

> Errors of speech are dangerous, he says, [but] far more dangerous are errors of the understanding. Therefore, we exhort you not only not to neglect the study of letters, but also with most humble mind, pleasing to God, to study earnestly in order that you may be able more easily and more correctly to penetrate the mysteries of the divine Scriptures.

As a result of his concerns, and through Alcuin, the emperor constructs an educational programme that changes the face of Europe for ever, not always for the better. The foundations of what could be called – rather grandly – the western European intellectual project are laid in a particular Christian conception of knowledge (penetrative and studious) and its importance to our relationship with God. But, as tends to be the case with foundations, they're no longer visible. And these days, in many church contexts, you are more likely to find emphasis placed on being loving rather than being right.

And you can discern a similar move away from the importance of knowledge in a good deal of secular thinking too. Take vegetarianism. In the late third century, the pagan philosopher and committed vegetarian, Porphyry (c.234–c.305) wrote a letter to his fellow philosopher, Firmus Castricius. Like me, Castricius has tried his best to go vegetarian, and failed. Porphyry takes him to task. 'I heard from visitors, Firmus,' he says, 'that you had condemned fleshless food and reverted to consuming flesh. At first, I did not believe it.' Firmus is in trouble. A few hundred pages of trouble.

These days, we tend to adopt vegetarianism, if not for environmental reasons, then because we know animals are able to suffer physically and emotionally. But that's not an argument Porphyry uses in his extended apology for a fleshless diet or, as we infelicitously put it these days, 'a plant-based lifestyle'. For Porphyry, the crucial point is not that animals can feel or have emotions or suffer, but that they can *think*. 'There is a rational soul in animals,' he claims, 'and they are not deprived of wisdom.' And that's why we shouldn't kill and eat them. As an example, he tells the story of Crassus, the Roman aristocrat who owned a pet lamprey, a sort of eel, which would come to him when he called its name. (Porphyry doesn't give the name of the eel unfortunately. Let's hazard at Larry.) When Larry the lamprey slithers off this mortal coil, Crassus goes into mourning. He doesn't serve Larry up in a parsley sauce.

Porphyry's objection to killing animals rests on our sharing a capacity with them to understand, to come when our names are called. Jesus uses understanding too, but contrariwise, as a way of distinguishing *between* human beings, between those with understanding and those without. Into which category do we fall? And can we cross from one to the other?

> 'When anyone hears the word of the kingdom and does not understand it, the evil one comes and snatches away what is sown in the heart.'
>
> Matthew 13.19

With the sower, Jesus offers us a parable in which the Word of God is represented as sown seed. Some seeds are pecked up by birds, others fall on thin soil, others are choked by weeds. But some fall on good ground and flourish.

The sower is effectively the parable of parables, a key that unlocks them all. It's not about knowing how to forgive, or knowing how to be neighbourly, or knowing how to be ready; it's about knowing how to know.

The parable is a picture of knowledge. Jesus tells us, if we wish the Word of God to take root and bear fruit in our lives, we cannot afford to stop listening; we must remain open to the Word, allowing it to grow through our lives. It is not a case of our penetrating the mysteries of scripture, as Charlemagne and Alcuin suggest, but of letting the mystery of scripture penetrate us.

The key to Jesus' theory of knowledge is a radical openness. Open ears, open eyes, open minds, open hearts. This is the purpose of the parable, the purpose of all true science and art: to wedge us open to change. We're not the grain; we're the ground. To understand is to be ploughed and harrowed, open and ready to receive.

.....

'THIS IS WHAT HEAVEN IS LIKE.'

These are Aggie's words. She's not gazing up at the Milky Way or standing on the edge of the Grand Canyon at sundown. She's entering a newly opened shop on the forecourt of a petrol station in a village near where we live. As well as sliding doors and air-conditioning, the shop boasts a milkshake machine and a hot dog dispenser; you can get slushies, frozen yoghurt and burgers to take away. While I'm pleased there's a new shop in the village, I don't yet feel its petrol pumps, post office counter and fast-food opportunities qualify it for celestial status. Why not? After all, Jesus compares mustard seeds and fishing nets to the kingdom of heaven. Why not a retail outlet?

You might think the answer depends on Aggie's intention, and Jesus'. Does she mean heaven will literally look like the inside of a Londis? I think she does. In which case, you'd be tempted to say she's not speaking metaphorically, whereas Jesus is. But is he? We presume there's a clear distinction between metaphorical and non-metaphorical language. But I don't think it's obvious where this boundary might fall, if there's a boundary at all.

A metaphor transfers the meaning of one term to another, ascribing to an object a property that it doesn't really have. Dawn doesn't break; night doesn't fall. When scientists say our brains are hard-wired in certain ways, they're speaking metaphorically; our brains aren't 'wired' at all. But nonetheless, we know what they mean. Likewise, if I say, 'Ben is a bear of a man', you know I probably don't mean Ben is covered in coarse hair, has sharp teeth and lives in the woods. For a metaphor to work, we need to be able to read contextual clues. You don't need me to spell it out: Ben is powerfully built, gruff, doesn't know his own strength, is prone to sulks, and so on. But there's a residue of meaning that can never be captured by my attempt to unpack 'bear of a man'. Like explaining a joke.

In order to function, metaphor is not simply swapping some words for others, or a game of comparisons. Metaphor requires us (impossibly) to share a whole world. The meanings of words shade off into an endless network of associations. When the psalmist says, 'The Lord is my shepherd', we're dropped into a matrix of meanings to do with leadership, care, protection, safety, and a recognition of our vulnerability. An entire description of humanity's relationship with God is conjured in those five words.

When Aggie asks me, as she regularly does, 'Do you believe in God?' or 'Do you think we go to heaven when we die?' I'm happy to answer 'Yes' and 'Yes'. But behind her question is a plea for proof that transcends language. I can't provide that. No one can. Not because God and heaven are *beyond* language, but because language simply doesn't work in that way. There is no non-linguistic stand-point available to me from which to view and assess our utterances. Even more challenging, perhaps there is no non-metaphorical standpoint either, in which case, meta-phor is not so much a figure of speech as the ground of speech. To say the kingdom of heaven is like a petrol station is full of meaning. To ask if that meaning is metaphorical is to suggest an alternative non-metaphorical description of heaven or petrol stations might be available. But what if there isn't, and language is metaphorical all the way down?

When Jesus is confronted by the crowds and Pharisees who are preparing to stone a woman caught in an adulter-ous relationship, he does something extraordinary.

> Jesus bent down and wrote with his finger on
> the ground. When they kept on questioning him,
> he straightened up and said to them, 'Let anyone
> among you who is without sin be the first to throw
> a stone at her.' And once again he bent down and
> wrote on the ground.
>
> John 8.6–8

Those unreadable words of Jesus' in the sand are, per-haps, the most important words in the gospel. Like the Pharisees, we often use language to construct customs, affirm traditions, establish laws, analyse the world, pin things down. We say what we mean, and we mean busi-ness. The certainty of the Pharisees and the 'righteous' crowd is built on the words they use, the arguments they can muster, the laws they're enforcing. But our longing still to read what Jesus has written in the sand and our inability ever to do so demonstrates how language and the things we build out of it are always under construction, effaceable in a moment, their meaning unstable, endlessly open to question.

When we use language to construct so-called necessary and eternal truths out of contingent and endlessly changing phenomena we inevitably fall into what the German playwright and thinker, Gotthold Lessing (1729–1781) called 'an ugly great ditch'. Too wide to cross and no ladder out. Our necessary and eternal truths turn out to be worryingly without foundations.

The way our curiosity to read Jesus' words in the sand is forever frustrated reveals how language must be shared from within. No one stands outside and gets to call the shots.

There's a petrol station on a roundabout off the A338, open twenty-four hours, and the coffee is free. It's heaven.

Tell me I'm wrong.

. . . . .

IT'S STILL EARLY, and no one else is up. Just me and the squatter. The window's open and I can hear birdsong, the muffled thud and whir of a boiler beginning to heat water for morning baths, and behind it all, the sibilance of a breeze in the beeches. It's quiet, but it's not silent.

I'm thinking about the sound of daily life, its pitch and intensity. I hardly listen to the radio these days. Or watch the news on TV. Living in a houseful of teenagers, I've learned to search for silence where and when I can. Trying to find space in the study to say Morning Prayer while the boys are in residence is increasingly difficult. Before settling down, I find myself having to collect beer bottles, Rizla papers, crisp packets and cereal bowls. But today I try not to tidy before Morning Prayer, but as part of Morning Prayer.

Working in the kitchens of his Carmelite monastery, Brother Lawrence sees menial tasks as an opportunity to practise the presence of God, not allowing himself to be confronted by the small things, but encountering God through them. 'We ought,' he says, 'not to be weary of doing little things for the love of God, Who regards not the greatness of the work, but the love with which it is performed.'

Amen: study and kitchen spotless. And I settle down to work in the quiet. The ring of the landline, the reversal alert of a recycling truck on the lane, a mobile vibrating on my desk, flies buzzing about in the lampshades. If I try to make silence a prerequisite for work, I'll never get anything done. But at the same time, it's worth remembering silence isn't the absence of noise, it's not emptiness, but a fullness, a presence. Kierkegaard tells us, despite the sound of the breeze, 'There is silence out there.'

> The forest is silent; even when it whispers it nevertheless is silent... The sea is silent; even when it rages uproariously it is silent. At first you perhaps listen in the wrong way and hear it roar... If, however, you take time and listen more carefully, you hear – how amazing! – you hear silence. In the evening, when silence rests over the land and you hear the distant bellowing from the meadow, or from the farmer's house in the

distance you hear the familiar voice of the dog, you cannot say that this bellowing or this voice disturbs the silence. No, this belongs to the silence, is in a mysterious and thus in turn silent harmony with the silence; this increases it.

It's a shame, I think, and indicative perhaps of our current obsession with being busy and distraction and noise, that the following verse from the ever-popular hymn 'Dear Lord and Father of mankind' is often omitted from modern hymnals:

> With that deep hush subduing all
> Our words and works that drown
> The tender whisper of Thy call,
> As noiseless let Thy blessing fall
> As fell Thy manna down.

In John Greenleaf Whittier's hymn, God's presence in the world is felt as a deep, subduing hush, as noiseless as a whisper. And it's our words and works, furiously filling the silence, that drown out God's 'still small voice' (1 Kings 19.12). We've ceased to know how to be quiet. We've forgotten the prophet Habakkuk's order 'Let all the earth keep silence before Him' (Habakkuk 2.20).

In one of his Christmas sermons, the Cistercian abbot, Guerric of Igny (c.1070–1157) invites us 'to hear the loving and mysterious silence of the Eternal Word speaking to us'. The paradox here isn't limited to the idea of a silent word. Guerric talks of a Word speaking to us. But words don't speak, they're spoken. This Word, it seems, is both speaker and spoken. And somehow silence too.

Like God, silence is limitless. Sounds come and go, yet they 'belong to the silence', as Kierkegaard puts it; silence stays. And like God, silence is utterly simple: it does not increase or decrease; it cannot be divided. Silence lies behind all sound; sound emerges from silence and returns to it. So silence is the opposite of absence; it is by virtue of silence that every sound is able to be present. And silence is ineffable: to speak about silence is to deny it, to oblite-rate it. It does not depend on anything else; it is underived.

And like God too, silence often goes unrecognised or unheeded, even actively rejected. The crucifixion was noisy. Silence is weak, useless, defeated. We have a right to remain silent, but we think it guiltily 'speaks volumes' nonetheless.

I once borrowed a book called *The World of Silence* by Max Picard (1888–1965) from a library in London. Years later, I came across a copy in a second-hand bookshop and bought it immediately. First published in 1948, it's almost completely forgotten now, and very hard to find, but it's full of wisdom and I highly recommend it. Picard says this:

> There is more help and healing in silence than in all the 'useful things'. Purposeless, unexploitable, silence suddenly appears at the side of the all-too-purposeful, and frightens us by its very purposelessness.

He describes silence as 'holy uselessness'. The silence behind the birdsong, the boiler and the breeze in the beeches is holy and healing in its very uselessness. I can put it to no use; rather, it puts me to use.

Still at my desk an hour later, I'm trying to write a sermon for Sunday's service on Zoom. And I'm at a loss. In the Church calendar, we've been through Passiontide and Easter; we've had Ascension and Pentecost. The story is over, and there's another six months or so until Advent and the story begins again. For the time being, we feel we're somehow outside the story. The Church calls this long period between Trinity Sunday and Advent Sunday 'Ordinary Time'. Not very inspiring. And yet, at the heart of the ordinary is the extraordinary. The ordinary emerges from the extraordinary like sound from silence. Maybe, instead of a sermon on Sunday, I should let the silence speak.

I fear Bertie the budgie might take that as an invitation...

.....

NINE-THIRTY, OR THEREABOUTS, I go outside to watch the orbiting string of Space X satellites. Turns out I've the time wrong, and they passed overhead an hour ago. But it's a warm night, with a nail-paring moon and Venus teasing the downs. So I stand for a while, looking up at the stars. When my neck begins to ache, I lie back on the grass, careful to avoid sheep shit, and the squatter comes to sit on my chest, gently rising and falling with my breath. She purrs.

It strikes me, after a bit, how the branches of the beech trees silhouetted against the heavens look like cracks, like dark 'spaces' or depths, when of course they're incalculably closer to me than the spill of stars beyond, way beyond.

I could almost reach out and touch the trees. Stars and galaxies, on the other hand, are unreachable. Sometimes we're drawn to what's unreachable, the intangible but twinkling, before we notice what's just in front of us. The stars feel so close I could lick them off the black, like salt. Each one differing from its neighbour. And the difference is the glory (1 Corinthians 15.41).

But I share far more with this tree into whose branches I'm looking: we're both made mostly of water, our genetic material is all but identical; and although we go about it differently, we both live by oxidising sugars and releasing their energy through respiration; we are both entirely reliant on our relationship with the environment around us.

Yet it's the stars, we feel, that hold the key to our future, while our past is locked in the rings of a tree's trunk. Lovers are star-crossed; we wish on stars. Family trees, by contrast are dead ancestors, done and dusty.

Trees are depositories, data dumps, sometimes literally: the bark of the beech tree in the spinney at the top of the down is covered in carved initials and dates.

The walnut by the flint wall in the manor garden was nearly uprooted in a storm, and we had to tension it back upright with ropes; the children used to hide in the hollow trunk of that enormous ash behind Mona's garden; and a sweetgum I planted with Nick in memory of Maisie has leaves just going gold. Theo's godfather gave us this gingko on his christening.

Trees call us home. But it's that very fact that leads to our overlooking them. It's their very remoteness that draws us to stars. Likewise, in our relationships with one another, it's always easier to spot the glamorous and glaring differences than the humdrum similarities.

Gregory Nazianzen, archbishop of Constantinople in the fourth century, wrote about our responsibilities to the poor and the sick in a sermon. He said we owe the poor, the destitute and the ill our kindness, our charity, not because of the differences in our stations or conditions, but because of the samenesses, because of what we share. It's not my having health or resources or position that requires me to reach out. On the contrary, it's the radical sameness of our underlying humanity that matters, that demands my helping. For Gregory, that sameness resides in our being made – all of us – in the image of God, and saved through the death and resurrection of Jesus Christ.

> For we are all one in the Lord, whether rich or poor, slave or free, whether healthy in body, or sick. And there is one head of all, from whom all things proceed: Christ. And as the limbs are to each other, so is each of us to everyone else, and all to all.

Modern philanthropy tends to start from another place altogether. It's on account of the (economic) differences between us that I have a duty to support you, help you, sponsor your exhibition, your play, endow your library. Or whatever. To illustrate, a passage from Jane Austen's *Emma*:

> It was sickness and poverty together which Emma came to visit; and after remaining there as long as she could give comfort or advice, she quitted the cottage with such an impression of the scene as made her say to Harriet, as they walked away, 'These are the sights,

Harriet, to do one good. How trifling they make everything else appear! – I feel now as if I could think of nothing but these poor creatures all the rest of the day; and yet, who can say how soon it may all vanish from my mind?'

Austen is able, almost as no other writer is able, to make us laugh at her characters even as we recognise ourselves in them. Austen is unsparing, yet humane.

Because, if I'm honest, I've found myself thinking like Emma Woodhouse recently. Every week, I take Joey and Theo with me to help deliver food boxes around the parish, to people who have lost their jobs and are struggling to make ends meet, or who are isolating and unable to get to the shops. It's good for the boys, I think, to talk to Gary and others, to see how different and difficult life can sometimes be.

See? Those are almost exactly Emma's words and thoughts. No, what the boys really need to see is not that people are leading different lives or different sorts of lives, but that we all belong to one another in the one life. We are not loved differently, valued differently or judged according to different criteria. God shows no partiality (Acts 10.34). And that doesn't entail a flattening out of our differences or the imposition of a stale uniformity or a barren equality. Rather, it means our differences do not divide us, but draw us together. We are called 'to care for orphans and widows in their distress' (James 1.27), to seek justice, rescue the oppressed and plead for the weak (Isaiah 1.17), not because our neighbours in need are divided from us by difference, but because they are united with us as limbs are to each other in a body, as branches of the same trunk.

.....

A FOX IS BARKING IN THE WOODS, plaintive and hoarse. The sound has a hopeless quality, and it's hard to tell where it's coming from. Close by, or down on the bottom fields? Or half a mile away across the valley?

I'm standing in the garden waiting for Aggie to return from an evening walk with her first boyfriend. They've climbed the hill to watch the sunset together. Who says romance is dead? I forget about the fox, and listen instead for Aggie's voice on the path leading down through the woods into the village.

It's getting dark. And I try again to arrange and order my feelings about my daughter having a boyfriend. Try again, fail again. I'm not good at change. I'm frightened of it still. The full moon rising out of the copse on top of the hill reminds me of Lon Chaney and his sideburns. What really frightens us about werewolves? They're us. We're all werewolves, changing, swept up in everything's changing.

In 1957, the Canadian literary critic and theorist, Northrop Frye, published *Anatomy of Criticism,* in which he identified a pattern in Shakespeare's comedies. He called this pattern 'the green world'. It goes like this: the characters in plays like *Two Gentlemen of Verona, A Midsummer Night's Dream* and *The Merry Wives of Windsor* begin in the 'real' world with all the usual Elizabethan rom-com dilemmas and predicaments; the plot then moves into a green world – a forest typically – where the characters undergo a series of trials and transformations, as a result of which lessons are learned, truths revealed. The characters return to the real world where all their earlier quandaries and confusions are resolved. Everyone gets married. The end.

The 'green world' offers us a way of accommodating ourselves to change by migrating it to a mythical elsewhere. Change (like the news) happens *there* so we can stay more or less the same and untouched *here*. Change is real, but removed, comes in bulletins and to other people. In part, then, these plays function as inoculations against change.

My daughter has a boyfriend, albeit a lovely boyfriend. But, nonetheless: *my daughter has a boyfriend.* Dusk accumulates under the trees and lengthens along the line of the hedge. Still no voices on the path.

Unlike Shakespeare's comedies where change is banished to a green world, change in the Bible is examined with ruthless, forensic honesty.

> As for mortals, their days are like grass;
>    they flourish like a flower of the field;
> for the wind passes over it, and it is gone,
>    and its place knows it no more.
>
> Psalm 103.15–16

But this change, while real and unavoidable, takes place within a context of a God who does not change (Malachi 3.6), whose love is everlasting (Isaiah 54.8), who is with us always (Matthew 28.20). The apostle James talks of the 'Father of lights with whom there is no variation or shadow due to change' (James 1.17).

We can't even begin to imagine what changelessness might look like or feel like, or even if the very notion makes sense. But that doesn't prevent John Donne from having a go in his famous prayer:

> No dazzling or darkness, but one equal light; no noise nor silence, but one equal music; no fears nor hopes, but one equal possession; no ends nor beginnings, but one equal eternity.

I confess it doesn't sound terribly appealing to me. Positively awful, in fact. Give me werewolves any day.

I check my watch again. Aristotle thought of time as an aspect of change, as a measure of change. I might sometimes think I'd like to freeze time – no ends nor beginnings – but if Aristotle is right, to freeze time would be to preclude change. And, despite our fears, we're called over and over again in the Bible to change, to be changed. To repent is to change your heart, and 'I tell you, unless you repent, you will all perish' (Luke 13.3). To change is to live, to be alive.

Aggie and her boyfriend return from their walk blissfully happy. Life moves on, changing, moment by moment.

Moments are marvellous, mainly, but it's their endlessly changing sequence through time which makes sense of them, and a story of us.

·····

I'M FED UP WITH MY FACE. On Zoom with colleagues, at school governors' meetings, leading online discussion groups or during Evening Prayer services – I check my chin, my hair; when did I last shave? I look tired and pale, I think; I look like a potato. No, I look like the ghost of a potato. Spectral tuber, spooky root veg: not a good look.

In an attempt to get away from the screen, from my own face, for a few hours, I went for a walk with Joey yesterday in Savernake Forest. Our destination was the King of Limbs, a sprawling, spread-eagled explosion of an oak, heaven knows how old.

There's an excellent, locally produced map of Savernake Forest. Our copy is sellotaped and folded into near illegibility, but that's immaterial: I left it behind on the dresser at home by mistake. And now I have only my vague memories of how to get to the tree, and a hopeless sense of direction to guide me.

After an hour or so of walking, we're not lost exactly, but I'm not a hundred per cent sure where we are.

I remember, as a child, being lost with my parents in the Grand Bazaar in Istanbul. Every corner looked the same, crowds pressing in from all angles. Gewgaws and rugs and garish fabrics, stacks of ceramic tiles, and fast-food stalls, then – off the beaten track, but still in the market – bicycle repair workshops, the racket of a clandestine commodity exchange down some back alley, games of chess and the sweet smell of apple-flavoured tobacco from hookah pipes, whole streets of spices. The deeper we went, the more lost we became. Until my father pointed to a window high up in the domed roof space. The sun slid in on a slant, dusty and dim. But, from the angle of the sun and a glance at his watch, he was able to work out which direction was north.

I still don't know how he did it, but he led us out of the bazaar in minutes, just in time to catch our ferry. That's a dad.

What isn't 'dad' is: sorry, I forgot the map, and I've no idea where we are.

But then Joey says, 'Hang on, let's take this path because I think... Yes, here it is.'

And there, suddenly, is the King of Limbs, a crashed and woody sputnik. A huge spider that's given up the ghost. I feel disorientated, a tiny bit un-dadded, my mental map of our whereabouts turning uselessly this way and that in my mind.

Savernake Forest is like the bazaar in Istanbul, a network, a complex and irregular web of paths and tracks. There's something chaotic about a forest, about a tree in a forest, just as there's something irreducibly chaotic about a market with all its myriad transactions and encounters. And I think our faith should be chaotic too: open and growing adventurously and perhaps bizarrely in odd directions, like the limbs of this tree. Capacious, home to all sorts of life.

The whole Modern or Enlightenment project has been 'categorial', an exercise in neatly parcelling up. Here's a map of the market, a map of the forest. Don't even think about venturing off it, because you can't. It's a bit like Zoom: everyone and everything in a box.

In one of her first published works of fiction (serialised in *Blackwood's Magazine* in 1857), George Eliot describes human societies, schools of thought and beliefs like this:

> Our subtlest analysis of schools and sects must miss the essential truth unless it be lit up by the love that

sees in all forms of human thought and work, the life and death struggles of separate human beings.

What Eliot recognises, it seems to me, is the protean, personal, shifting, maze-like nature of human relationships at the heart of our organisations. If our faith is neat, all rules and rituals and generalisations, kept for church on Sundays, it's no faith at all. In his letter to the Philippians, St Paul describes himself as

> circumcised on the eighth day, a member of the people of Israel, of the tribe of Benjamin, a Hebrew born of Hebrews; as to the law, a Pharisee; as to zeal, a persecutor of the church; as to righteousness under the law, blameless.
>
> Philippians 3.5–6

Blameless, he's on the inside. He can  pinpoint himself on the map. And feel entirely secure as to his place in the world and in the eyes of God.

But that's all crap, as he admits himself:

> I regard [all that] as rubbish (*skúbala*, literally 'dung') in order that I may gain Christ and be found in him, not having a righteousness of my own that comes from the law, but one that comes through faith in Christ.
>
> Philippians 3.8–9

To be found in Christ, as Paul puts it, is to be lost to righteousness according to the law, an outlaw, literally, and off the map. It is, instead, to be lit up by the love that sees and knows the life and death struggles of all human beings.

Faith is not one stall among many in the market. It can't be reached by following a map. It breaks in, through a high window – from outside. It's a sudden turn down a different path.

.....

A FRIEND LIVING IN LONDON UNDER LOCKDOWN took to posting pictures of the city on Instagram. It was shocking to see familiar streets suddenly, eerily empty. Without people, the city had taken on that 'museum' quality you find at archaeological sites. These buildings, streets and thoroughfares, you feel, had a function and a life once, but quite what it was and what it was like you can no longer remember or imagine.

In one photo I recognised the junction of Waterloo Bridge and the Strand, where the Strand becomes Aldwych. There's the Lyceum, with its posters still up for *The Lion King*. And not a single person to be seen.

It's an apocalypse, I thought. Or rather, it's what we call an 'apocalypse'. Apocalypse has become familiar to us these days, primarily as a cinematic genre. But of course, it's really a biblical term referring to a form of literary, prophetic writing. In Greek, the word 'apocalypse' means an uncovering, an unveiling. Or revelation. The last book of the Bible, the book we call *Revelation*, is – in Greek – *Apokalypsis*.

Biblical apocalyptic writing is rich in the poetics of waiting, of longing for redemption, for freedom, for a

Christ. In our day, 'apocalypse' means not waiting for the cause of our renewal, but facing the effects of our failure to renew ourselves or our world. Biblical apocalyptic looks forward to the future; in modern, cinematic apocalyptic there's no future to look forward to.

Bridging the gap between modern and biblical meanings of apocalypse is a song. 'Morning Dew' was written in the 1960s, during the Cold War, by a Canadian folk singer called Bonnie Dobson. It's a simple song about the aftermath of a cataclysmic event. Only two people on the planet are left alive, a reversal of the Eden myth.

The song was made famous by the Grateful Dead, who regularly included a rambling version of it in their live sets. Towards the end of May 1972, the band were playing several concerts at that same Lyceum Theatre on the Strand in London. Warner Brothers were paying to have these concerts recorded for a live album. But in characteristically chaotic style, there was only one sound engineer working in a Heath-Robinson-style van-cum-studio parked outside the theatre. One particular evening during that run at the Lyceum, this engineer realised, to his horror, that there was a problem with a piece of equipment on stage. Being on his own, he had no choice but to leave the precious tapes running unattended in the van on a busy street while he went inside to fix the issue.

Now, the Dead were quintessentially a live band; they never played the same song in the same way twice. Improvisation, freeness and play were the band's modus operandi. So, if you missed it, you missed it for ever.

During their version of 'Morning Dew' that night, the band's lead guitarist, Jerry Garcia, caught sight of the sound engineer, and he knew in that moment there was no one at the sound desk; there was obviously a major problem with the recording. Perhaps there *was* no recording. What did he do? Garcia smiled mischievously at the engineer, turned in on himself and poured his heart into a sublime, unrepeatably beautiful solo, often considered one of the most transcendent moments in contemporary popular music – *and no one was at the controls.* And more: Garcia knew no one was at the controls.

Interviewed many years later, the sound engineer wept as he recalled the depth and playful beauty of Garcia's action that night. Luckily for us (and for that sound engineer), the tapes were perfect and the recording ended up on *Europe '72*, all twelve celestial minutes.

Of course, the coronavirus pandemic is not an apocalypse in the cinematic sense or in the 'Morning Dew' sense. But perhaps it *should* be an apocalypse in the biblical, in the Garcia sense. Faced by this crisis, the sense that the tapes are running 'unattended', that a disaster is unfolding, what should we do? Like Garcia that night at the Lyceum, perhaps we should trust, turn away from the shallow, superficial, self-conscious world of our own making and recording, and open ourselves instead to revelation, playing our hearts out, as if no one's listening but God.

And while we're on the subject, let's rescue the word 'recording' from the recording industry. The Latin for heart – *cor, cordis* – sits at the centre of our word 'record'. Etymologically, to record means, not to preserve or to render reproducible, but to have by heart. A recording *can be* a reel of tape, or an mp3 – it'll sound the same every time you press play. Or a recording can be a miracle. Something which changes us, re-hearts us, like Garcia's playing, or like feeling the throb of Mahalia's singing 'He's got the whole world in his hands'.

God says to Ezekiel, 'I will remove from your body the heart of stone and give you a heart of flesh' (Ezekiel 36.26). You can record by carving on stone: deeds, facts, laws, commandments. But you can only really record in a heart of flesh.

.....

WE'RE KEYWORKERS. Emma breaks the news as she comes off the phone to the NHS Covid-19 helpline. That teachers are keyworkers strikes me as uncontroversial, but vicars? Unlike Emma, nothing I've done over the last few months has been key to anything or anyone. Still, I'm not complaining. We're eligible for testing. Yesterday evening, Nick's wife, Lissa, rang to say she'd tested positive. We'd all gone walking together the week before, up Golden Ball Hill to watch the sunset.

Emma, Aggie and I pile into the Ibiza and set off for a testing site just off the M4.

Sporting hi-vis vests and medical-grade masks, staff check the Ibiza's number plate against their lists and wave us onto the site where nurses stand and wait outside temporary huts. For a moment, these nurses remind me of off-duty fighter pilots from films like *The Battle of Britain*, where 'the chaps' sit around in goggles and bomber jackets, smoking pipes, drinking brown tea and brown beer and cracking off-colour jokes. The nurses aren't smoking or drinking tea. They aren't in bomber jackets either, they're in scrubs – gowns, gloves, visors.

Winding the Ibiza through endless lanes of traffic cones, I begin to feel the Covid-19 testing process is like a cross between an advanced driving test and wandering onto the set of a disaster movie.

All the hyper-hygiene and efficiency of the testing facility serves somehow to emphasise our vulnerability, the precariousness of our situation. All this, you can't help thinking, on account of a submicroscopic infectious agent with a canny ability to replicate itself plentifully in our mucous membranes. We're being invaded, colonised. This place is the frontline. The nurses are like fighter pilots after all, and this a Biggin Hill in a new Battle of Britain. A battle we're losing, according to the nightly figures for infection rates and death tolls. To think, just six months ago, I thought R was a letter of the alphabet.

Before Lissa rang with her positive bombshell, I was putting a Zoom service together. And the collect prayer for Sunday is still fresh in my mind as the nurse in full PPE approaches my car window, signalling. 'Would you wind your window down for me, please?'

> O God, the protector of all who trust in thee,
> without whom nothing is strong, nothing is holy:
> increase and multiply upon us thy mercy
> that, thou being our ruler and guide,
> we may so pass through things temporal
> that we lose not our hold on things eternal;
> grant this, O heavenly Father,
> for Jesus Christ's sake our Lord,
> who liveth and reigneth with thee,

in the unity of the Holy Spirit,
one God, now and for ever. Amen

One of the glories of Archbishop Cranmer's 1549 Prayer Book are the collects, the prayers for each Sunday. Some he composed himself, most he translated from the Latin of the Sarum Breviary into his peerless Tudor English.

I look past the nurse's plastic gown, and open my mouth wide. Ahhhhhh.

And I think about that 'protector of all who trust in thee'. We've all been taking precautions, keeping our distance, wearing masks, showing up for tests, washing our hands. (There's a particular supermarket brand of coconut-scented soap that comes in fiddly pump-action dispensers and which Emma, feverish with Covid, bulk-ordered back in March. When all this is over, I know that sickly chemical approximation of 'coconut' will linger as a dreadful Proustian trigger, immediately able to plunge me back into the long days of lockdown.)

While we act on government advice and doctors' instructions, while we may hope these measures will prove preventive, we don't, it seems to me, put our *trust* in them. Nor, if we're honest, do we put our trust in those who've formulated these measures. Where do we put our trust? The answer can't only be in see-through plastic and scented soap products. It's a bigger question demanding a bigger answer.

Trust is a form of faith, and contrary to how the word is often used, faith is not only something we have, or lack; it is something we do. So, St Augustine reminds us, 'Faith is not what one believes but what one believes with.' Like love, it only works when given. We're encouraged these days to trust in ourselves, to have faith in ourselves. But surely that's like Baron Münchausen pulling himself out of the swamp by his own hair: a joke. It can't be done.

The test is uncomfortable. Aggie and Emma don't baulk for a second at having an elongated cotton bud jabbed around their tonsils or stuffed up their noses. Of course, I'm hopeless, gagging and sneezing and generally embarrassing myself.

Test completed, we 'pass through things temporal', the remainder of the test site, twisting round and round its cordoned intestines, to the exit where we all breathe a sigh of relief. And as we peel off the spur onto the empty motorway, that line in the collect comes back to me: 'without whom nothing is strong, nothing is holy'. It can be read, I realise, in a couple of ways. It could mean, some things are strong and holy because God ensures they are strong and holy. Or it could mean, outside God nothing is strong or holy; but *in* God, everything is.

Over and over again in the Psalms, God is described as a refuge, a stronghold, a tower, a fortress. God is not so much a who as a where.

You who live in the shelter of the Most High,
    who abide in the shadow of the Almighty,
will say to the Lord, 'My refuge and my fortress;
    my God in whom I trust.'
For he will deliver you from the snare of the fowler
    and from the deadly pestilence.

Psalm 91.1–3

My trust, my faith – whether I put it in God or a vaccine or the nurse – is always an acknowledgement of my weakness, my abiding need for a fortress, for shelter, for a refuge. And in that acknowledgement is my salvation. 'For whenever I am weak, then I am strong' (2 Corinthians 12.10).

.....

THE SWAN has been a grocer's shop, a takeaway, a food bank, a delivery service, all in the space of six months. But it's on the point of reopening as – wait for it – a pub. Much as I'd love to support the Swan in its new/old capacity, Emma reminds me, we're still isolating.

Like the pubs, churches are considering how they might open again. This week, All Saints' has opened its doors for private prayer. Going in for the first time in nearly half a year, I was struck by how the building seemed to welcome me back, as though it had been waiting. These buildings are patient.

Almost immediately, just twenty-four hours after unlocking the doors, I was sent a video by Joy, the church-warden, of three boys running amok in the aisles, chancel and side chapels. Pretty harmless stuff actually, just the sort of thing bored boys are likely to get up to given half a chance and having been hemmed in at home for months on end. Of course, Joy knows the name of one of the boys and so I'm duty bound, I suppose, to pick up the phone for a difficult conversation with the parents. I'll do my best to reassure them: no harm done. But the incident has raised questions in my mind about openness.

All Saints' is open again and therefore open to being abused. And if you think about it, the boys were open too, openly sharing their video on social media (which is how Joy ended up seeing it). Foolish on their part, but telling in its own way. Openness, a willingness to share, is always foolish, risky. As a result, our instinct is often to close up, even in the way we think. We parcel up the world to our advantage, neatly, in boxes. And in so doing, we enslave ourselves to all sorts of prejudices and dogmas, habits and traditions because it makes us feel stronger, safer. As Nietzsche grimly recognises, slavery offers us what we really want. 'The slave wants what is unconditional; he understands only what is tyrannical, even in morality; he loves as he hates, without nuance.' Spend time scrolling through Twitter, watching *Question Time*, or listening to the rabid radio phone-ins on Radio 5 and you'll see what Nietzsche means. Subtlety or nuance leaves a chink open; we don't want that; it's weak, vulnerable. We admire unyielding strength and certainty. You draw a line, and you defend it at all costs. You see it in our politics; you even see it in our landscape. Recently, every entrance to every field, every gap in the hedgerows around the village, has been blocked by a felled tree or a trailer bed or a low metal gate, padlocked. Surveillance cameras mounted on barns and grain silos lend the village a 'Private: No Entry' aspect. They're there for a reason. Hare-coursing has gone from being a niche (and nasty) blood sport to big business around here. Webcast from mobile phones, the chases attract large audiences of gamblers all over the world. With huge sums at stake, the hare-coursing gangs are not likely to be the older brothers of those boys in All

Saints'; they'll be armed, professional criminals.

The danger is that in defending the line, in policing the border, you find the border comes to define you. You don't draw the line; the line draws you.

The parables of the New Testament and the prophecies of the Old are not only open, they're unclosable, their meaning endlessly nuanced, endlessly elusive and deferred, running amok. No reading is definitive. It is a truly open text. As Jesus says, 'If you continue in my word, you are truly my disciples; and you will know the truth, and the truth will make you free' (John 8.31–32). Knowing the truth is not, for Jesus, to do with having facts at your fingertips, or even being right; it is a setting free. The Word of God does not have a full stop after it. And yet, idolatrous, we put our faith in laws, written codes, instructions; we love tyranny; we choose it. In Dostoevsky's novel, Ivan Karamazov says,

> I tell you, man has no more agonising anxiety than to find someone to whom he can hand over with all speed the gift of freedom with which the unhappy creature is born.

Canny demagogues understand this instinctively; freedom is the last thing people want. Ivan in the novel offers us a parable in which Jesus is made to stand trial again before the Grand Inquisitor. The Inquisitor accuses Jesus of betraying the true interests of human beings. 'Instead of taking possession of men's freedom you multiplied it and burdened the spiritual kingdom of man with its sufferings for ever.'

The Grand Inquisitor is right. Freedom and the truth are a burden to us, they make demands on us and entail suffering. Jesus' life and death are testament to that. Occasionally we glimpse the truth, a glimpse of true, loving, risky openness and it frightens us. We prefer the tyrannical, the campaign slogan and soundbite, prefer to listen to the Pharisee with his rules and laws and traditions, prefer to be told what to do and how to think.

'I promise they won't do it again, vicar,' says the boy's dad on the phone. God, what have I become? A slave, a Pharisee? Once I was one of those boys. And I pray, even as I speak on the phone, that I might retain just a pinch of their openness, their foolishness, their play.

As we prepare to open our buildings – churches, mosques, synagogues, temples (and our pubs) – we must prepare to open ourselves too.

God,
wholly uncontainable,
Creator, Redeemer, Sustainer
eternal Father of our Lord Jesus Christ,
to whom no door is closed, nothing hidden,
dig up our worlds of convictions and certainties,
break in on us in the midst of our fear and anxiety.
When we thirst for evidence – have mercy on us
when we crave certainty – have mercy on us
when we make demands – grant us peace
through your Risen Son our Lord
standing in the midst of us.
AMEN

.....

BACK AT MY DESK, WITH A HEADACHE and feeling tired, I wonder: are these symptoms? And as I search the drawers of the desk for old packets of ibuprofen and crumpled sachets of Lemsip, I happen to glance down the new garden path. There's movement by the shed. Not unusual. I think it must be someone delivering a parcel. But then I notice this character has picked up Joey's bike, which was propped against the wooden slats of the shed, and is making off with it through the gate and out onto the lane where a car is parked.

Notwithstanding my headache, and without thinking, I jump up, throw myself down the stairs and out the front door. Barefoot, I dash along the path, shouting and hopping about on the sharp stones.

By the time I reach the lane, the car is thirty yards down the road opposite the stable yard.

'Hey, that's my son's bike!' And I throw in a few blunt Anglo-Saxon terms for good measure. The car stops. Not what I'd expected. And a man emerges. A big man.

'Leave the bike there,' I shout, bravely, as he pops the boot and begins to pull out the bike. I assume he'll drop it and drive off. But he doesn't. Instead, he climbs onto the bike and cycles up the lane towards me.

I'm going to get in a fight here, I think, strangely calm. When was I last in a fight? At school. And I lost that, quite badly. One of my front teeth is false. Another scar. Memories surface suddenly, of scrapping in the lunch queue, opening my bloody mouth for the nurse in the 'san', sitting outside the headmaster's office; the unsympathetic clattering of a secretary's typewriter.

'Heber-Percy!'... Gulp.

The man is just a few yards from me. My neighbour, the farmer, lives right there, I think, trying to reassure myself. I glance at his door. It's the middle of the afternoon. Someone will have heard the shouting, surely? And so, my panicky thoughts run on as this man cycles towards me.

When he's close, a few feet away, he steps off the bike, wheels it through the gate and puts it back quite carefully where he'd found it. And as he walks past me again, our eyes meet briefly, then he sets off down the lane to the car. I say nothing, lost for words.

My model for Christian life is not Christ himself, or not directly. That strikes me as entirely impossible, altogether beyond me. My model, the pattern according to which I try to live my life, is Monseigneur Myriel, the bishop of Digne, a fictional character from the opening chapters of Victor Hugo's *Les Misérables*. Those chapters describe a man who 'overflowed with love' who has 'a serene benevolence embracing all men, and extending even beyond them. He lived disdaining nothing, indulgent to all God's creation.'

When the hero of the novel, Jean Valjean, a released convict, an outcast, shows up, desperate, at the bishop's door, he's told, 'Come in'. Valjean has previously been rejected from every inn and hostel in the town. The bishop welcomes him, feeds him and treats him as a valued guest.

In the middle of the night, unable to help himself, Valjean helps himself to the bishop's silver and flees the house. He's pursued and caught by the gendarmes and dragged back to Digne and the bishop. When the gendarmes present the 'crushed and woebegone' Valjean, the bishop exclaims:

> 'So here you are!... I'm delighted to see you. Had you forgotten I gave you the candlesticks as well? They're silver like the rest, and worth a good two hundred francs. Did you forget to take them?'

This story of infinite kindness, of Christlike, unworldly generosity mixed with mischievousness, has had a gravitational effect on me over the years. It's acted like scripture, like a compass.

Not enough, it seems. Look at me in the lane, watching this stranger slouch back to his car. I could've asked if he was alright. I should've let him have the bike; after all, I have others. I have everything. I feel utterly hopeless and ashamed of myself.

At least I've learned how quickly and completely the world's values can assert themselves and take hold when you're not thinking, when you're frightened or angry. That's mine. Give it back. And yet my Lord says, 'If anyone strikes you on the right cheek, turn the other also; and if anyone wants to sue you and take your coat, give your cloak as well' (Matthew 5.39–40).

Bishop Bienvenue, as he's known to the people of the town where he works, has lived up to Christ's injunction to welcome the stranger, to clothe the naked, to feed the hungry: 'Truly I tell you, just as you did it to the least of these who are members of my family you did it to me' (Matthew 25.40). I didn't do it.

Lord, have mercy.

.....

NEXT MORNING, I wake to the sound of text messages pinging through the house. We've all tested negative. I neck a few more ibuprofen, just for good measure, and raise a cup of Lemsip. I'm still feeling rubbish.

After saying a thankful Morning Prayer in St Michael's, I sit for a while. Stained red, violet and green by saints and angels in the windows, the light shimmers and drifts over the floor and grey walls. The air is cool, like evening, and smells of polish and candles. Our neighbours, John and Sylvia, keep these pews gleaming. There's a bottle of their homemade polish – a secret recipe, John winks – in the vestry cupboard. Occasionally I unscrew the lid, press my nose close and take a deep hit before walking up the aisle for an 8am Holy Communion: an astringent blast of lemon and beeswax and something petrolly. Clears the sinuses.

*Dearly beloved brethren...*

In my prayers today, I remember Iris, as I often do, a parishioner and friend I've known for many years. Her husband is buried in the churchyard outside, a few metres from where I'm sitting now. He's been there thirty-four years. Iris has planted primroses and anemones around his headstone.

I went to visit Iris recently. Two metres apart, we sat in her garden, shaded by an old English rose. Although her short-term memory is failing, she vividly recalls planning the garden with her husband when they first moved here from London. Digging the borders, planting trees, opening up views across the downs. The terrace is a scramble of daisies.

At the end of our conversation, we fall naturally into prayer. And although she struggles to find the right words in our chats, Iris still has the Lord's Prayer perfectly by heart.

On the way home, I stop off at the Swan. Not because it's lunchtime and hot and I fancy a pint. (All true.) But because I've been given a list of things to buy by Aggie. Top of Aggie's list is flour.

Though Bill, the landlord, is in the process of reopening his pub, the bar is still propped up by sacks of potatoes, and covered with punnets of carrots, onions and parsnips. And flour: self-raising, plain and strong. When shelves in the home-baking sections of our supermarkets stood empty, Bill spotted a demand. He sells eggs too, milk, yeast and vanilla extract. Hundreds & thousands, and those little edible silver balls.

Like many others, Aggie, who hasn't been in school for weeks and weeks, has taken to baking. Every afternoon she's in the kitchen, apron on, dancing and cooking to her Classic 80s playlist: Madonna, Hall & Oates, Toto, Dexy's, Spandau... the list goes on. And on.

Despite my lingering headache, I can just about forgive the music in order to watch her making lemon drizzle sponges, marble cakes, banana loaves, cardamom-scented 'boller' buns, macaroons.

It strikes me while I'm watching her: here's the reason for Jesus' using bread so often and so crucially in his thinking. From the growing of the grain to the milling, to the sharing of the loaves, bread is a process.

When Jesus says, 'I am the bread of life' (John 6:35), I don't think he only means that he is our sustenance, that he alone can satisfy our hunger; I think he means to offer us a complex, rich, fruitful life to be led and shared. Life like cake.

When Elijah begs the widow at Zarephath for some bread she tells him,

> 'I have nothing baked, only a handful of meal in a jar, and a little oil in a jug; I am now gathering a couple of sticks, so that I may go home and prepare it for myself and my son, that we may eat it and die.'
>
> 1 Kings 17.12

But at Elijah's urging, she bakes him bread and finds her little store of flour and flask of oil endlessly replenished. Again, I don't think this is just about Elijah, the widow and her son being kept miraculously alive; it's about sharing, responding to the needs of others, even in the midst of our own need. And read in that light, the widow's words above are a recipe. Not for bread, but for salvation.

Even with the kitchen window open, the smell of baking fills the whole house. Before they've finished cooling on wire racks, I've wolfed a cupcake or a Chelsea bun or whatever Aggie's made. Born with a sweet tooth, I've managed to cut out chocolate. Or nearly. I still buy the occasional Bounty. But I can actually justify that on professional grounds. The little white cardboard inserts serve very well as make-do dog collars when you've forgotten to put one in before leaving the house. I took a funeral once with a Bounty Bar dog collar neatly in place. The mourners were none the wiser.

Aggie and I spoon out sweet dough mixture from the

mixing bowls. Jesus describes the kingdom of God as being like yeast mixed through flour (Matthew 13.33; Luke 13.21): all around us all the time. And through the story of our lives, we're mixed together, folded into one another. The yeast is essential: there's no such thing as self-raising people.

·····

DUST IN THE AIR, grain lorries in the lanes, and thunder flies in my hair: harvest is here. The roads are clotted with tractors pulling huge cutting platforms from one field to another. And the hot nights are full of thirsty, rumbling combines.

I'm trying to change the blades on my lawnmower which was a gift from my parents many years ago. Mower propped up on logs, I lie on my back in the long (and lengthening) grass and weeds. The first two bolts loosen easily enough but the last won't budge. When the spanner slips, I bark my knuckles on the mower's metal skirt. So I take a blowtorch to that third and final nut in an effort to heat it off the bolt's rusted thread, and I start chiselling away, lifting nibs of bright steel until it gives. Inelegant, but effective.

Later, in the vestry and changing into my cassock for a funeral, I find my socks and the backs of my trousers are covered in burrs from where I was lying in the grass trying to fix the mower. Around here these burrs are called beggar's buttons. I pick them off one by one and drop them out the vestry window. And think no more about it.

This will be the first service held here since March, and

Joy and I are out of practice. I'm trying to remember how to fit fresh batteries into the lapel mic when I hear a shriek in the nave, and rush out to find Joy with smoke pouring from her head. She's set fire to her hair while lighting candles on the altar. I frogmarch her to the basin in the vestry and press a wet towel to the burning patch.

Joy studies her hair in the mirror. No damage done, she says, that a judicious comb-over can't disguise. But the church smells of burnt hair throughout the funeral, lending proceedings an unhelpfully infernal quality.

Unable to sing together, we sit, masked, listening to Joy play (rather shakily, it has to be said) through 'Morning Has Broken' on the organ. And despite my concerns for Joy, I remember how I saw dawn break this morning when I let the cat out, and heard the first birds. What does it mean to say morning has *broken*? Does the day break in the way my mower keeps breaking?

In the story of the feeding of the five thousand, Jesus breaks the bread in order to share it out. The story occurs in all four gospels. Although there are slight variations in each telling, all four mention the grass on which Jesus tells the crowds to sit. I love the way Mark specifies that the grass is green. In John's gospel 'there was a great deal of grass in the place' (John 6.10), which just makes me think of my broken mower back home sitting on what was once a lawn. Perhaps I could claim to be rewilding?

Each of the gospels is careful to describe the bread collected following the miracle as broken, as fragments. 'And all ate and were filled; and they took up what was left over of the broken pieces, twelve baskets full' (Matthew 14.20). The brokenness of the bread is important.

Mornings and loaves, I realise, are similar inasmuch as they're breakable. And being breakable, they're shareable. A morning is shared: we all wake into it, move through its light; a loaf of bread can't be eaten alone; it must be shared among friends, with the hungry. And we break and share our hearts too. I look out at the eyes above the masks in the congregation. Their hearts are broken for the person with whom they've shared so much.

It's easy to imagine ourselves as the crowds who've followed Jesus out to this deserted (albeit grassy) place to hear him and be healed. But perhaps we're being asked to see ourselves in the bread, broken and left over, fragments to be gathered up. That, I think, is the living truth of the miracle of the feeding of the five thousand and the reality of the kingdom of God: to live fully is to be broken open and shared out, Christlike, given and then gathered.

Joy draws the hymn to a close. We all stand to go outside for the committal. When the family have left, I stay behind to chat to Joy, to check she's not still smouldering, and to thank her for playing. She lends me a treasured Greek grammar for Theo, who's off to university in a fortnight or so. Last of all, I close the window in the vestry and lock it. And I pause. This time next year, I wonder, will there be a huge clump of giant burdocks growing where I dropped those burrs from earlier? It occurs to me then, immediately after the funeral, and having laid to rest a loved mother, grandmother and friend in the ground, why there's such an emphasis on brokenness in the miracle of the feeding.

'Very truly, I tell you, unless a grain of wheat falls

into the earth and dies, it remains just a single grain;
but if it dies, it bears much fruit.'

John 12.24

We come into the world to be broken, to be shared.
Sometimes, in our arrogance, we're able to convince ourselves we move alone and heroic through the world, but
the truth is quite the reverse: God's world is constantly
moving and growing through us, sharing itself, telling
itself, scattering itself all the while, in love.

.....

AS I WALK OUT OF ALL SAINTS' into the sunshine, I
remember the two butterflies I rescued months ago from
where they were trapped, fluttering against the east window. I notice many more butterflies now, as I make my way
back to the car.

Later, walking up the hill to clear my head, there are
butterflies everywhere – painted ladies, holly blues and
brimstones – their shadows flickering on the path in front
of me. This year, the ways are full of midges and crickets
sawing away to themselves among the tall grasses, sedges
and seed heads of drying cow parsley. The air is thick with
insects, and later it'll be flickery with feasting bats.

Compared to golden fields of wheat or swaying barley,
the rapeseed crop in the top field looks scruffy, out at the
elbow. And among the rape are patches of barley blown in
from elsewhere. Not weeds, but not wanted either.
'Volunteers', I'm told they're called, these refugees from the
field across the way. I love that. Volunteers suggests they're

here willingly; they set sail and landed here, and I can't help seeing them as settlers, pioneers.

In 1969, British philosopher, John Wisdom (1904–1993) published an influential paper in the *Proceedings of the Aristotelian Society* entitled simply 'Gods'. In it, Wisdom describes a thought experiment in which two men come across a neglected garden. Some plants are flourishing, still fruitful, and one of the men suggests the garden is tended, cared for by a gardener. His friend points to all the weeds and dilapidation; he believes the garden is wild.

They decide to test their contradictory hypotheses, and set up watch. When no gardener appears, and none of the neighbours have seen a gardener at work, the sceptic's hypothesis looks the more likely. But the believer argues that the gardener comes at night, while they're asleep. Or perhaps the gardener is invisible.

Wisdom's point is that both parties are able to claim support for their beliefs by reference to evidence already before them: the beauty of the garden, the diversity of flora, the air of artful abandonment or actual abandonment; and no new evidence is forthcoming.

> Each learns all the other learns about the garden. Consequently, when after all this, one says 'I still believe a gardener comes' while the other says 'I don't', their different words now reflect no difference as to what they have found in the garden, or would find in the garden if they looked further.

The son of a clergyman, and himself a Christian,

Wisdom does not think the two characters in his story disagree about empirical facts. Their argument is over differing perspectives regarding those facts. And he believes we come across disputes like this all the time, not just in arguments over whether or not God is at work in the world. He uses the example of how we share our views on art, or reach a decision in a court of law. Hearing someone describe why they love a particular piece of music or a painting might – or might not – lead to our own appreciation. Sitting in a jury room, and hearing the views of others who have listened to the same evidence and testimony, can – quite reasonably – alter or confirm our views as to the guilt or innocence of the defendant. In both cases, the facts remain precisely the same.

> 'The kingdom of heaven may be compared to someone who sowed good seed in his field; but while everybody was asleep, an enemy came and sowed weeds among the wheat, and then went away. So when the plants came up and bore grain, then the weeds appeared as well.'
>
> Matthew 13.24-26

Where Wisdom's thought experiment and this parable coincide beautifully is in the prominence given to ignorance, of definitive proof being unavailable to us. In the parable, the enemy comes when everybody is asleep. In Wisdom's thought experiment, the believer argues that the gardener comes at night, unseen.

'And the slaves of the householder came and said to

him, "Master, did you not sow good seed in your field? Where, then, did these weeds come from?'"

Matthew 13.27

Look around, there are weeds. The world presents itself to us as a morally equivocal landscape. From one perspective it seems like a beautiful garden; from another it looks wild, untended. Like the slaves in the parable, we don't know where the weeds come from. And we might even differ as to what constitutes a weed in the first place. I'm looking at volunteers of barley in a field of rapeseed. A few yards away, over that fence, this barley would be crop; here it's weed. If I'm a red admiral or a tortoiseshell butterfly, a nettle isn't a weed, it's home.

The decision we make as to what is worthless weed and what is valuable crop will depend on context, and on judgement. And all the while we're called to grow alongside one another, our root systems too closely entwined to pull up the weeds without damaging the crop: 'In gathering the weeds you would uproot the wheat along with them' (Matthew 13.29).

More pressing still, perhaps *we* are weeds, volunteering as such, or unintentionally. Or maybe sometimes we're weeds, sometimes cherished crops. What to do in this situation? Jesus' parable offers an eminently practical position: we must grow together for the time being. Where the weeds came from and what will become of them are questions we can ask and about which we can have reasonable opinions, like Wisdom's sceptic and believer in the garden, but the truth will only come at harvest.

'The harvest is the end of the age, and the reapers are angels. Just as the weeds are collected and burned up with fire, so will it be at the end of the age. The Son of Man will send his angels, and they will collect out of his kingdom all causes of sin and all evildoers, and they will throw them into the furnace of fire.'

Matthew 13.39–42

Until then we can only look on ourselves, on one another, and on the ambiguous world of which we're a part, in expectation, in trust: that a gardener comes.

Almighty God,
may we be sown, grown and brought home
in your Son.
AMEN

# MUSIC

**LYING IN BED WITH THE WINDOWS OPEN – PAGE 83**
'Conference of the Birds', Dave Holland Quartet, *Conference of the Birds* (ECM, 1973)

**MERVYN – PAGE 89**
'Air', The Incredible String Band, *Wee Tam* (Electra, 1968)

**TURN THE IGNITION – PAGE 92**
'The Theme from Starsky and Hutch', The James Taylor Quartet, *Live at the Jazz Café* (Real Self Records, 2008)

**IN ITS BATTERED STATE – PAGE 96**
'Get Down Moses', Joe Strummer and the Mescaleros, *Streetcore* (Hellcat, 2003)

**PLAGUED BY A HARE – PAGE 98**
"Out of Egypt, into the Great Laugh of Mankind, and I shake the dirt from my sandals as I run', Sufjan Stevens, *Illinois* (Asthmatic Kitty/Secretly Canadian and Rough Trade, 2005)

**A NEW AGGRESSIVE FRONT – PAGE 101**
'John Barleycorn', traditional, Traffic, *John Barleycorn Must Die* (Island, 1970)

**THIS IS WHAT HEAVEN IS LIKE – PAGE 106**
'Soul Alphabet', Colleen, *Captain of None* (Thrill Jockey, 2015)

**IT'S STILL EARLY – PAGE 109**
'Immunity', Jon Hopkins, *Immunity* (Domino, 2013)

**NINE-THIRTY OR THEREABOUTS – PAGE 113**
'May the Circle Remain Unbroken', 13th Floor Elevators, *Bull of the Woods* (International Artists, 1969)

A FOX IS BARKING IN THE WOODS — PAGE 117
'Moments in the Woods', by Stephen Sondheim, Emily Blunt, vocalist, *Into the Woods, Original Motion Picture Soundtrack* (Walt Disney, 2014)

I'M FED UP WITH MY FACE — PAGE 119
'In a Persian Market', Albert Ketèlbey, John Fahey, *Old Fashioned Love* (Takoma, 1975)

A FRIEND LIVING IN LONDON UNDER LOCKDOWN — PAGE 123
'Morning Dew', The Grateful Dead, *Europe '72* (Warner Brothers, 1972)

WE'RE KEYWORKERS — PAGE 126
'Oomingmak', The Cocteau Twins, *Victorialand* (4AD, 1986)

THE SWAN — PAGE 130
'Going Through the Veil – Becoming a Swan', Joanna Brouk, *Hearing Music* (The Numero Group, 2015)

BACK AT MY DESK, WITH A HEADACHE — PAGE 134
'Happy Cycling', Boards of Canada, *Music Has a Right to Children* (Warp, 1998)

'Forgiveness', Rachel's, *Selenography* (Quarterstick, 1999)

NEXT MORNING — PAGE 137
'Only You', Yazoo, *Upstairs at Eric's* (Mute, 1982)

DUST IN THE AIR — PAGE 140
'New Grass', Talk Talk, *Laughing Stock* (Verve, 1991)

AS I WALK OUT OF ALL SAINTS' — PAGE 143
'A Love Supreme, Pt. IV – Psalm', John Coltrane, *A Love Supreme* (Impulse, 1965)

# AUTUMN

STORMS ROLL THROUGH ALL WEEK, and the last of
the harvesting takes place in between. We're past the equi-
nox, a tipping point, and frosts are around the corner. The
hedgerows are full of blackberries and bright hips, and the
blackthorns along the lane are blue with sloes. Apples,
pears, plums and damsons: the haul this year will be spec-
tacular. Somehow, though, there's a portentousness in the
bowed branches, the mornings full of mist and the falling
leaves. Heading into winter still in the grip of a pandemic
is an alarming prospect.

Spring is a series of glimpses; autumn envelops you.
And the season always seems to have a curious double
aspect; it's a time of preparation, of new terms and fresh
starts. But it's also shot through with melancholy and a
sense of looking back, of taking stock, nostalgia. This year,
both directions offer views of steep climbs, long roads,
peaks and troughs. It's been a year of graphs. Next slide,
please.

Iris has been moved to a care home in London. We still
meet once a week, but now on Zoom, to say prayers and
to talk. Her Polish carer sets up the laptop for her. This
week Iris wants to talk about her childhood in Yorkshire
and the Scottish Borders. Born in 1923, Iris remembers
the Second World War vividly. She talks about how, as a
child, she'd never want to say goodbye to people. 'You

never knew,' she says, 'if it might be really goodbye.'

I drove Theo to London this week, the Ibiza packed to the tatty fabric headliner with boxes and bedding and his bonsai in the mouldy passenger foot well. He's off to university. I found his halls tucked away in a street off Gray's Inn Road. Together we unloaded the car, and lugged boxes and bags up four flights of stairs.

One of the last jobs Theo did for me before leaving home was build a bonfire in the garden: dry leaves and fallen ash branches and pulled-up courgette plants. Standing together, with the squatter curling around our legs, we watched the tower of smoke rising up through the cold, clear air. And thousands of sparks, twisting into the dusk. They reminded me of this verse from Job:

> Human beings are born to trouble
> just as sparks fly upward.
>
> Job 5.7

.....

ALL THE BRANCHES OF THE APPLE TREES in our garden are clustered with fruit. Red and green, too tart for eating still, but it won't be long before they swell and soften and sweeten around the seed.

Last autumn, Theo had a Saturday job at a local apple-pressing business. People bring their apples from all around; just a car boot-full, or an entire orchard. The fruit is pressed into juice, bottled, sterilised and labelled. The business is run by Richard. I remember Richard remonstrating once with an eccentric Australian churchwarden who admitted to resorting to reiki to help with her back-ache. Richard said he didn't trust alternative therapies and chose to rely on his GP and the Holy Spirit. 'Listen, mate,' said the churchwarden waspishly, 'I take what I can get.' I rather admired her practical, pick-'n'-mix approach.

Theo would come home from a day's work smelling of cider and cheap Romanian cigarettes he'd bummed off Jonel, who worked there with him. This year, by the time apple pressing begins in earnest and help is needed in the yard, Richard will find Theo unavailable, flown the nest. Theo will miss the work, and I'll miss collecting him on Saturday afternoons. Come to think of it, I'll just miss him. He's the apple of my eye.

The apple of my eye – it's a phrase with which we're all more or less familiar. The expression crops up several times in the 1611 King James Version of the Old Testament and is adopted in most subsequent translations. The psalmist petitions God to 'Guard me as the apple of the eye; hide me in the shadow of your wings' (Psalm 17.8). Breaking unexpectedly into glorious song at the end of Deuteronomy, Moses thanks God for sustaining Jacob (Israel).

> In a desert land,
> in a howling wilderness waste;
> he shielded him, cared for him,
> guarded him as the apple of his eye.
>
> Deuteronomy 32.10

And the Lord says to the exiled Hebrews that 'one who touches you touches the apple of my eye' (Zechariah 2.8).

In each of these cases, the word used in the Hebrew, then in the Greek and Latin translations, is the word, not for apple, but for the pupil of the eye: *korē* in Greek, or *pupilla* in Latin. 'The apple of my eye' is an *English* idiom. The early seventeenth-century translators of the Bible into Jacobean English used a colloquial term for the pupil of the eye, and because of their translation's enormous influence, the phrase has been in popular currency ever since.

But it's not quite as straightforward as that. The English translators would have known that both *korē* and *pupilla* are not strictly ophthalmological terms. *Korē* and *pupilla* are words clustered and grafted with a jumble of meanings and associations. In both Latin and Greek, the words for the pupil of the eye also mean 'little girl', 'daughter' or 'maiden'. In short, the translators have recognised that the psalmist and the prophets and the writers of the Old Testament are themselves using idiomatic, poetic language; Moses and Zechariah are not referring literally to the pupil of the eye. For them, as for us, to talk about the pupil of the eye is to talk about something dear, something loved and precious. Something like Theo.

I love how language does this. Not because it points to the peculiar brilliancies of English or Latin or Greek or Hebrew. Rather, because it points to a failing in all language. Language can't ever capture the world perfectly; there's always a residuum, an inarticulable left over. Every locution is a circumlocution; my words are never precisely on target. How could I possibly capture exactly what it feels like for me to pick Theo up from work on a Saturday afternoon, express my love for him? Language as a structure, as a system fails, but its failure is its glory. By failing, it is constantly reaching for the residuum, circling never seizing, steering a course between reference and nonsense. To talk about the daughter of my eye, the girl of my eye, the apple of my eye is nonsense, as Lewis Carroll knows well.

> The Red Queen shook her head. 'You may call it "nonsense" if you like,' she said, 'but *I've* heard nonsense, compared with which that would be as sensible as a dictionary.'

Precisely, your majesty. Dictionaries are sensible, a way of trying to make language obedient, ordered, on target. But language has an innate tendency to the skew-whiff, to disorder, to run away with itself and us. Meanings proliferate. A simple phrase like 'the apple of my eye' can refer to a part of my body, *and* to something infinitely precious to me, while remaining – strictly speaking – nonsense: my eye has no apple. The dramatist and poet, Antonin Artaud (1896–1948), talks about language as an 'uprooting of thought, a revolt, a labyrinth of unreason, not a dictionary into which the pedants who dwell on the banks of the Seine direct their mental contractions'.

Using the language of poetry, parable, prophecy and the apocalyptic, the Bible consistently denies contraction, but insists on expansion. It uproots our easy codes, definitions and rules; like language itself, it never lets us settle. As such, it is not like a sensible dictionary, but more like an uprising, a demand. It gestures beyond itself, points to the curved horizon of language, a Word.

Look up the word 'dictionary' in a dictionary. Dictionaries

are circular, more or less arbitrary abstractions. We can grow apple trees and compile dictionaries, but sometimes we need reminding: agriculture is not creation, and dictionaries are not language. You won't find the Word of God in a dictionary. Rather, all possible dictionaries are in the Word of God. It's this Word, this horizon, that Christians believe 'became flesh and lived among us' (John 1.14). As a beloved Son, as the apple of someone's eye.

> Creator God,
> Speaker of the Word through whom all things are made
> > and Father of a beloved Son,
> we give thanks for the richness of your creation,
> and the mystery at the heart of all things.
> By your Holy Spirit, inspire us always to try to measure the immeasurable,
> > to determine the indeterminable,
> > and to fail, but fail beautifully.
> And all the time, draw us further along the Way, deeper into the Truth,
> > and more richly into the Life of your Word,
> our Lord and Saviour Jesus Christ.
> AMEN

.....

STARGAZING AGAIN; it's Perseid season. But off in the distance a storm flickers, as if the night's gone on the blink. And the sky is busy with bats. I climb the hill for a better view. Through air still hot and thick with harvest

dust, towering blooms of cloud far to the north are inter-
mittently lit up from inside – apricot and smudged ochre
and amethyst.

It reminds me of an illustration in the first prayerbook I
owned. My parents gave it to me for my ninth birthday. I
still use it regularly. One of the five or so colour plates
included in the book (unhelpfully halfway through the
Eucharistic prayer) is a painting of the Israelites at the foot
of Mount Sinai. They are worshipping the golden calf, a
Baal, a god of Canaan. Up on the mountain, God's anger
at their apostasy is depicted in flashes of lightning and
tumbling dark cloud: 'Now let me alone, so that my wrath
may burn hot against them and I may consume them'
(Exodus 32.10).

A few years ago, I worked with a writing partner on a
commission to adapt a novel by John Buchan for the
screen. Famous for *The 39 Steps* and *Greenmantle*, Buchan
is revered in Scotland, not for his thrillers and adventure
stories, but for *Witch Wood*. Set in the lowlands of Scotland
during the seventeenth century and published in 1927,
*Witch Wood* is Buchan's best novel by a long chalk, in my
view. It tells the story of a newly ordained and idealistic
young minister, David Sempill, who finds himself called to
an isolated parish stewing in hypocrisy, religious sectarian-
ism and superstition. It's set in a harsh landscape of forests
and hills, cut off from surrounding communities by plague,
snow and war. (Not the most encouraging depiction of
rural ministry, it has to be said.)

At one point, in an excess of righteous fervour, Mr
Proudfoot, a member of David's congregation, utters this
wonderful line:

'Let us see that there is no Canaanitish thing in our midst,' Mr Proudfoot cried, 'for the purge of the Lord is nigh. And let Israel dwell in unity, for a house divided shall not stand.'

Strict Presbyterians, Mr Proudfoot and his fellow Covenanters wish Scotland to be a theocracy, free of kings and bishops, a commonwealth under God and God alone. They see Scotland as Israel. And a Canaanitish thing could be a golden calf, a king or a candle. No infringement of their code or their authority will be tolerated. (By the way, 'Canaanitish' may qualify as my favourite adjective of all time.)

To think in terms of Israel and Canaan, as Mr Proudfoot does, is to divide the world between right and wrong, friend and foe, in and out, us and them. So it's not built on unity, as Proudfoot believes, but on a binary view. The language of 'Canaan versus Israel' is the language of the border. It's a language that runs deep in us all. It's the language we use to define ourselves. The purity of the Presbyterians derives ultimately from the popish impurity (as they see it) of their foes. Likewise, jihadists are not only motivated by their opposition to the kafir, they *exist* on account of their opposition to the kafir. The Orange Walks in Ulster persist because of the Catholic streets through which they pass. The *raison d'être* of the Ku Klux Klan is the African American. And so on.

The contemporary Italian philosopher, Giorgio Agamben, notices this pattern across all human societies. He says, 'that which is excluded from the community is, in reality, that on which the entire life of the community is founded'. Ultimately, Dr Frankenstein is as much a creature as the thing he sews together on the slab in his laboratory. More, he is the creature's creature.

The followers of Jesus twisted this idea in a radical way, not defining themselves over and against what they rejected, but identifying themselves *with* the rejected, as Jesus does, seeing himself as the Suffering Servant described by Isaiah:

> He was despised and rejected by others;
>     a man of suffering and acquainted with infirmity;
> and as one from whom others hide their faces
>     he was despised, and we held him of no account.
>
> Isaiah 53.3

This foundation-deep association with the rejected, the excluded and the unacceptable presents Christianity with a challenge. Christians can't pretend to be strong, armoured against their adversaries: they're called to love and forgive them. They can't hide behind rules, or borders, or boundaries because they're already and always beyond the pale.

In the district of Tyre and Sidon, when Jesus encounters a Canaanite woman who pleads with him to cure her daughter, he first ignores her and then says, 'I was sent only to the lost sheep of the house of Israel' (Matthew 15.24). When she continues to beg him to help, he snaps at her, 'It is not fair to take the children's food and throw it to the dogs' (15.26). 'Yes, Lord,' the woman agrees. 'Yet even the dogs eat the crumbs that fall from their masters' table' (15.27).

A woman, a gentile, outside the faith tradition, rebuked

and rejected, is able to respond boldly and faithfully, unde-
terred. Jesus says to her, 'Great is your faith.' Faith is about
stepping across a border.

At the end of *Witch Wood*, David Sempill is excommuni-
cated at a rigged trial on trumped-up charges. His friend
stands up before the 'righteous' congregation and accuses
them of being Pharisees. "'It's nothing but a bairn's ploy,"
he cried, "but it's a cruel ploy, for it has spilt muckle good
blood in Scotland.'" It has spilt much good blood the
world over: our faithless tendency to barricade ourselves
behind terms like Israel and Canaan. What Jesus and the
Canaanite woman together reveal is the truth behind the
bairn's ploy, behind the lies of political rallies and headlines, behind our own prejudices. Unity can so easily
become an idol, a false god, a Baal. The border between
Israel and Canaan is real; it's how you *respond* to the border that counts. To cower behind it, as Proudfoot does,
misusing words like 'unity' is faithless. True faith, it seems
to me, is having the courage, like Sempill in Buchan's
novel, or Jesus and the Canaanite woman in the gospel, to
step out from behind the big words, and across the border.
After all, the point of a border, ultimately, is its crossability.
An uncrossable border isn't a border.

When Jesus prays to his Father in heaven that his
disciples 'may become completely one' (John 17.23), the
unity he's praying for is a much more radical notion than
the Proudfoots of this world can imagine or accept.
Proudfoot's version of unity is divergence: them *from* us,
right *from* wrong, Canaan *from* Israel. Jesus' unity is con-
vergence; it's a coming together.

The Canaanite woman serves to illustrate this coming

together; she is an interruption, a breaking through. Perhaps that's the essence of a living faith – it interrupts.

. . . . .

HERE'S AN UNCHARMING SNATCH of doggerel you occasionally hear repeated around here:

> *Wiltshire born, Wiltshire bred,*
> *Strong in the arm, thick in the head.*

It expresses the same sentiment as a story well known in these parts. One night, a visitor to the county comes across a group of Wiltshire men busy trying to rake the moon's reflection out of a dew pond. On being questioned, the locals claim they're hoping to fish this big cheese out of the water.

A home-grown variant of the same legend casts the visitor as a customs and excise officer, and the Wiltshire rustics as smugglers who had hidden barrels of French brandy in the pond. Spotted by the officer, the locals played dumb with a fanciful tale about the moon, and some cheese. Not so thick in the head after all.

Either way, there's a pub in Pewsey, just down the road from where I live, called the Moonrakers in their honour. Truth be told, the Rakers, as it's affectionately known to locals, is probably not a pub in which you'd expect to bump into the vicar. There's a dancing area, I hear, with a pole. The Rakers has a reputation. Mind you, Pewsey itself has a reputation.

According to legend, in the ninth century, when Alfred,

king of Wessex, went off to do battle with the Vikings, he left his wife in the care and custody of the good people of Pewsey. Following his victory at the Battle of Edington (878), he returned to Pewsey to find his wife safe and well. As a reward, Alfred granted the people of the vale the right to an annual feast around the time of Holy Cross Day.

Devoted to the exaltation of the Cross on which a blameless yet provocative Galilean was put to death around AD 33, Holy Cross Day maps the shocking theological territory occupied by Christianity: a faith that takes as its central symbol an instrument of torture. A means of murdering a human being in the most humiliating and debasing way imaginable becomes the site of our salvation, the means of our redemption. It's from this place that Jesus Christ is able to promise paradise to a thief being crucified next to him (Luke 23.43). For Christians, the nadir is the apogee, the last shall be first, weakness is strength, the stone rejected by the builders becomes the cornerstone of the temple. We are built from brokenness.

Alfred's ancient feast is now part of Pewsey Carnival which was first held in 1898 and has grown to become one of the largest annual street parties in south-west England. I love Pewsey Carnival. Everyone does, except perhaps the local constabulary. It's mayhem, but it's glorious mayhem, all super-strength cider, cannabis and candy floss, chips with curry sauce: more English than Elgar. King Alfred would approve: this is us with our Saxon roots showing.

The carnival opens and closes in worship. Several times I've led a service with hymns accompanied by a brass band on the hardstanding outside the fire station and opposite

Alfred's statue. And every year, at dusk on the night of the parade, Aggie and Anwen pull on their wellies, wade out into the shallow chalk stream that runs through the village and help light candles. It's not easy work. The candles sit in antique coloured-glass lanterns suspended on a loose lattice hanging a few feet over the stream. The girls are given little spills of wadding pre-soaked in butane and attached to a thin metal wire. Each candle has to be lit individually, and there are many, many hundreds of them. But to light them is to be part of something quietly beautiful. As daylight fades, the candles in the glass lanterns begin to shine like stars, and their reflections shiver and twist through the running water below. A moment, still yet moving, simple yet full of complexity: just light and water, and love. It's a prayer.

And then comes the raucous, thumping train of marching bands and floats on trailers stacked with precarious sound systems and pulled by tractors. Beery, garish and unhinged, the procession weaves and lurches through the village.

But not this September. Carnival has been cancelled for the first time since the 1950s, when Britain's agricultural heartlands were being ravaged by another virus – foot and mouth disease. Aggie is desperately disappointed. She's convinced she saw her first dead body at Pewsey Carnival one year. Just outside the fairground site, she says. Dead drunk is more likely, but you never know with Carnival.

It's easy to feel cast down. But therein lies the deep meaning of Holy Cross Day: the kingdom of heaven is in the midst of us. Redemption, like the reflected lights of coloured lanterns, is perpetually present over the rushing surface of our lives if we only stop to look, and salvation always looms behind the mundane, behind disappointment and change. What looks like loss, brokenness, is actually the means of our salvation. What appears to spell disaster actually presages victory. For the women standing at the foot of the Cross, this wooden structure is not a symbol, not a sign; it is devoid of meaning, something that sucks meaning out of the world. A black hole. The end of the story.

And yet, over the course of two thousand years, that Cross has transformed from a disaster, to a hopeful, wild secret shared among a handful of disciples, to a universal symbol of love worn around the necks of countless millions, topping off towers and steeples and domes across the world, a gesture made over the bodies of Christians everywhere, smeared in oil on the foreheads of our babies, and on the hands of our dying. It is the way into the world, and the way out of it. Christians are people of the Cross. And that means standing, in the words of Simone Weil, 'at the intersection of creation and its Creator. The point of intersection is the point of intersection of the arms of the Cross'. The nail of the Cross, she goes on, 'has pierced cleanly through all creation, through the thickness of the screen separating the soul from God'.

We may not know what the future holds, but Christians have faith through the Cross. Like the robber nailed next to Jesus, we have a promise. Live in it.

Live nailed to it.

. . . . .

BONE-SHAKING AT THE BEST OF TIMES, the Ibiza's suspension takes a pounding on this particular drive. We're bouncing along the Grand Avenue, a long straight track that bisects ancient Savernake Forest, and I'm giving Joey a driving lesson: pulling away, emergency stops, hill starts. So, it's not just the suspension that's complaining; the gearbox too, and the exhaust is starting to sound throaty.

Teaching a skill that's second nature means having to think about actions and movements to which I normally pay no attention. Coming to a stop, do you engage the clutch before putting your foot on the brake? I find myself using my feet to answer the question for me. My feet know, my brain doesn't. It's disconcerting.

We keep things hidden from others, of course, for countless reasons. But we keep things hidden from ourselves too, sometimes out of expedience, sometimes because we're frightened of snagging on an old pain. But there are aspects of ourselves we keep covered up simply because they've become muscle memory, ingrained habits and behaviours we no longer think about. They're automatic.

Driving is a habit of this sort. Faith is another. Or can be. Now and then it's helpful to hit a pothole or snap a fan belt. It forces you to pop the bonnet and peer inside, to get your hands dirty again, or burned.

Outside, the air is close and we hear thunder occasionally over the revving engine. Check the mirror, indicate, brake, then clutch. We pause at an intersection in the middle of the forest to enjoy the last of the sunshine.

Handbrake.

Above us, the leaves are shivering greens and golds

against the featureless deep blue of an approaching storm. We climb out of the car to stretch and breathe; the air is almost fizzy with ozone.

I pull driving to bits in order to see how I do it. Pulling faith to bits to get at the fundamentals is worthwhile too; questions raised in a confirmation class or a school assembly are often harder and more penetrating than those from delegates at a conference or students in a seminar. They force you to think again about the foundations, about what's been buried by habit.

In the fast lane of a motorway, driving a modern, silent car with adaptive cruise control and advanced driver-assistance systems, it's easy to forget – in all the quiet and comfort – the speed and power of the vehicle. Faith can become comfortable too. You can take your feet off the pedals, hands off the wheel. You can nod off.

Cars are designed to divorce us from the messy and dangerous business of internal combustion. Perhaps everyone should drive an Ibiza now and again, to remind themselves: it's noisy, dirty and dangerous. And, like the Grand Avenue, the Bible is helpfully rutted with potholes. Here's one:

> 'Whoever loves father or mother more than me is not worthy of me; and whoever loves son or daughter more than me is not worthy of me.'
>
> Matthew 10.37

You need your feet on the pedals here, and both hands on the wheel. Suddenly, we have to concentrate. I'm being asked to weigh my love of God against my love for this boy beside me in the car. And I love him desperately. My every instinct tells me to skirt this pothole. I don't want to hit it, address it. So, can we avoid the difficult Matthew passage, dismiss it as an anomaly? Here's Luke:

> 'Whoever comes to me and does not hate father and mother, wife and children, brothers and sisters, yes, and even life itself, cannot be my disciple.'
>
> Luke 14.26

Even worse! This pothole is un-skirt-round-able. Perhaps we should just remain silent about such passages. But commenting on this exact verse, Kierkegaard points out, 'silence is only a futile evasion'. And furthermore, he says, any tasteful watering-down, or clever exegetical she-nanigans designed to lessen the impact of Jesus' words 'ends up in drivel rather than terror'.

> The words are terrible, but I feel sure they can be understood without the person who understands them necessarily having the courage to do as they say. And yet there must be honesty enough to admit what is there, to confess to its greatness even if one lacks the courage oneself. Anyone who manages that will not exclude himself from a share in the beautiful story.

We may not be able to live by these precepts, he's saying; we may believe we *oughtn't* live by these precepts. But let's be honest about what's there. Potholes are real.

Through honesty and confession, Kierkegaard suggests,

we are granted a share in the story. This is a profoundly important insight. The centrality of confession and honesty to the way Christians live out their faith is a process of endlessly placing potholes before ourselves, getting our fingers burned, falling short, striving to make ourselves worthy of this story, and refusing to allow faith to slip back into 'automatic', to become second nature. We need to remember we're not Porsche Cayennes, but Seat Ibizas: hopeless, unreliable, but loved.

The Bible is rutted and twisty, useless as a means of confirming our own biases and prejudices; it is constantly wrong-footing us, interrupting us. It is not an instruction manual, or the Highway Code. It's a text in which to live. And every life, like every good story, is bound to be full of ups and downs, scenic routes, sudden reverses and dead ends.

For a time, before I was ordained, when the children were young and I was working as a screenwriter, my route through life seemed straightforward. Or if, on occasion, I came across a diversion or a crossroads, there was always a signpost, someone helpful to ask directions who'd been this way before. The road was smooth. Or smoothish.

One night, I was up late, working on a script for the History Channel, when the phone rang. It was Nick. I heard the panic in his voice straightaway; he was struggling to speak. Between sobs, he asked me to pray. Please pray for Maisie, he said. Pray for her.

His daughter, Joey's best friend, a girl of twelve, had suffered a brain aneurysm and was being airlifted to hospital. Over the phone, I could hear the helicopter's rotor blades behind where Nick was standing.

Emma was beside me in her dressing gown. We grabbed a torch, left the children sleeping and walked to the church. We lit a candle and sat in the dark. And prayed.

Two weeks later, Maisie died.

And you still believe in God? someone asked me at the time.

All stories, as every screenwriter is always being told, depend on jeopardy. But jeopardy in turn depends on preciousness. Without preciousness there's no jeopardy and without jeopardy there's no story. Preciousness is at the heart of any story, like the seed, the grain, the pearl. To be worthy of this story, as Deleuze puts it, to be worthy of our lives, we have to embrace the preciousness, grow around the preciousness.

Jesus' demand that we hate our fathers and mothers, daughters and sons reminds us of the terrible preciousness at the centre of our lives. When God commands Abraham to sacrifice his son, Isaac, the threat to remove preciousness reveals it, cracks us open. No one hears that story without *feeling*, viscerally, what preciousness is. For Abraham, Isaac has not just been born, been loved, been saved; he's been returned.

> Isaac said to his father Abraham, 'Father!' And he said, 'Here I am, my son.'
>
> Genesis 22.7

Spending those weeks and months – years – with Nick and Lissa and their family, a family I love, a family suffering unendurably, I glimpsed, I think, the preciousness of preciousness. There were moments that marked me for ever. I saw Lissa saying goodbye to her daughter through the wicker lid of a coffin.

I sometimes think God doesn't love us. God *lives* us. And if we're prepared to say, 'Here I am', to love whole-heartedly, to run that risk, then we live God.

And living like this costs. The potholes are real. And the story is beautiful, not despite the 'terrible' words, but somehow because of them. If everything were precious, then nothing would be.

We hear it first, the rain coming towards us through the forest. Drops, warm, the size of gobstoppers, in the leaves above us, all around us, suddenly. Soaked to the skin in seconds, Joey and I rush back to the Ibiza. Before he can open the driver's door, I hug him to me.

Inside, catching our breath, we watch the rain running down the windscreen like tears, like all the tears, and we listen to it hammering on the roof. It's beautiful, Joey says, and he smiles across at me.

Here I am.

Clutch. Gear. Accelerator.

.....

IN TERMS OF ELEVATION ABOVE SEA LEVEL, St James' is the highest church in the diocese, or so I'm told, sitting tucked into the lap of the hills, surrounded by ancient yews.

I park the Ibiza at the end of a track and enter the steep churchyard by a metal gate, sunlight sliding in on the glance, gold. The early-morning air is vaporous and vaguely boozy with the scent of windfalls. All around me, the din of cockerels and lambs and children in the distance. Apart from the chill, and the dew underfoot, if I close my eyes I could be back in Africa.

I'm due to lead a Holy Communion service here this morning, my first since March. I'm nervous.

Richard, the churchwarden, arrives soon after me, swinging a 1980s executive-style attaché case. I follow him inside the church and watch as he places the case carefully on the altar and flips the catches. Nested in grey packing foam, like parts of a rifle, are an ancient silver chalice, paten and ciborium. He lifts the items out one by one.

Before the service begins, we gather in the churchyard to sing Charles Wesley's hymn, 'Love divine, all loves excelling'.

Then, back inside, we light candles – not ceremonial here; necessary. St James' is without electricity. And gradually, in the pews, people congregate, become a congregation. From people to *a* people. Communion begins at the door, not at the table.

I prepare the altar, re-familiarise myself with the feel of freshly ironed linen, the way light catches and curves on polished silver surfaces, the sound of wine poured into the altar jug, the soft spill of communion wafers. So much of what we do in Christian worship engages our bodies, our senses. Before theology, before ideas, before all the words, Eucharist is a physical experience. The body sits at the centre of the sacrament:

> Though we are many, we are one body because we all share in one bread.

Broken pieces, we are made whole again by sharing in him who was broken for us all. And this is not done by magic or a miracle; it's done by a meal. Bread, wine, water. Friends. The Eucharist is not doctrine, or shouldn't be; it's dinner.

When it comes to the familiar prayer that recalls Christ's words at the Last Supper, I raise the paten and then the chalice into the light and tell the story again, for the first time in many months:

> In the same night that he was betrayed,
> our Lord Jesus Christ,
> took bread and gave you thanks;
> he broke it and gave it to his disciples, saying:
> Take, eat; this is my body which is given for you;
> do this in remembrance of me.

So much that's happened recently has felt like a coming apart. Not only are we asked to isolate from our neighbours and friends, we are asked to *self*-isolate. It's hard to know quite what this means. But it makes me think of the items in Richard's briefcase, each separated from the others, slotted into its own discrete foam niche. When we're cut off from one another, we're cut off, in a real sense, from ourselves, dismembered. Here, now, we're put back together. This is remembrance, a re-membering.

As I lift the paten, it occurs to me that Jesus *gives* three times in the space of a single sentence. He gives thanks; he gives bread; he gives himself.

And as the congregation comes up to the altar rail, one by one, it's not the sacramental theology that counts; it's these people, these friends at this table, receiving that which is given.

George Eliot writes in *Middlemarch* that, 'There is no general doctrine which is not capable of eating out our morality if unchecked by the deep-seated habit of direct fellow-feeling with individual men.' The Eucharist is not, as I say, a doctrine, but a demonstration of a deep-seated habit of direct fellow-feeling.

And afterwards, up on the track that runs along the top through fields of stubble, I pull over to look out across the valley. Shreds of mist still clinging in the draws and hollows, and all the villages just waking. And I realise, I'm lost. Not lost as in I don't know my way home, but lost in the way Wesley puts it in 'Love divine' – I'm lost in wonder, love and praise.

·····

DRIVING BACK INTO THE VILLAGE, I have to wait for the grain lorries trundling along the lanes. In recent years, the farmer has built a huge new barn. Ever since I had to rescue my brother's cat from an empty grain dryer when we were boys, I've had an aversion to modern farm buildings. There's something about the swept concrete, the wide apron of hardstanding and the unlovely galvanised metal superstructures that depresses me. Trapped in a cooling duct where the air was thick with dust, the cat's eyes were glued up when we found her, and she could hardly breathe. In my arms, as we crawled out of the silo, she was skin and bones, half-starved. We'd been searching for her for days.

Since the squatter's arrival and my reintroduction to 'pet life', I've thought a lot about my brother's cat and how we rescued her. I've recalled how much we loved her, how precious she was to us, how we built a nest for her out of an old cupboard when she had a litter of kittens.

On account of my experience in the grain dryer, I have a sort of sympathy with Jesus' censuring of the farmer who says, 'I will pull down my barns and build larger ones, and there I will store all my grain and my goods' (Luke 12.18–19). But my disapproval of the farmer in Jesus' parable can stretch only so far. I mean, what's he really done wrong? Whatever my personal feelings about barns, here's a man, like my neighbour, who has worked hard, prepared and planned ahead. And yet…

'God said to him, "You fool! This very night your life is being demanded of you. And the things you have prepared, whose will they be?"'

Luke 12.20

To many of us, these words might seem particularly harsh this year. A small but noisy convoy of tractors ground along Marlborough High Street the other day. They were protesting beacause the local MP had voted against a House of Lords' amendment to the Agriculture Bill, which would have protected British farming from cheap imports from countries with lower food safety and animal welfare standards. In the midst of a pandemic, we feel the need for a secure and safe supply of local food. Farmers feed us. More than ever, they require our support and our understanding, not our criticism. And yet Jesus goes on.

'Consider the ravens: they neither sow nor reap, they have neither storehouse nor barn, and yet God feeds them.'

Luke 12.24

Should we do nothing then? Is that what our protesting farmers should do? Put their feet up? Is this a parable for the work-shy, for the idle? As always, there's a danger of reading the parables morally, or even politically, when I think they're to be read existentially. We can't absorb these texts; they absorb us. So, the parable of the rich farmer isn't about the point or pointlessness of planning and preparing and working; it's certainly not a text about land management or agricultural policy. It's about waking up to a new truth, a completely different way of being in the world.

Immediately before the parable, Jesus warns his followers:

'Take care! Be on your guard against all kinds of greed; for one's life does not consist in the abundance of possessions.'

Luke 12.15

Get this wrong, Jesus is saying, assume your life consists in your possessions, and it's not that you'll be breaking the rules, that you'll be punished, or that you'll be in sin. In the truest sense, you won't even be alive.

And a few verses after the parable of the rich farmer, Jesus tells his followers: 'it is your Father's good pleasure to *give* you the kingdom' (Luke 12.32). You can't earn the kingdom. You can't work for it or work your way into it. It's a gift to you from a God who takes endless pleasure in giving, whose essence is giving and loving.

Like my brother's cat in the grain dryer, we can so easily find ourselves trapped and blinded in our own worldly ways of thinking, in vast structures that seem to have no exit. Jesus' parables are glimpses of a way out. Light in the darkness.

.....

THE NIGHTS ARE DRAWING IN. Every year we set ourselves a challenge: not to turn on the central heating in our cottage until the beginning of Advent. Some years, if I'm honest, we've not made it. Emma's complaints grow bitterer than the cold in the bedrooms, and I give in. By my reckoning we've another five weeks to go, and the temperature is dropping. But there are mitigations. So many ash trees have died in the last couple of years, we have a seemingly endless supply of seasoned firewood. And then there's the cooking. For reasons I can't explain, autumn always encourages me back into the kitchen. Perhaps it's the abundance of squashes, mushrooms and game in the shops.

To keep the cold out, I start to muck around making soups, stews and casseroles. Food to keep us warm. There are favourite recipes, easily found because the pages in the books are all food-splattered and scrawled over with notes. Recipes become a way of indexing the time of year. We triangulate our position in the calendar by recourse to certain repeating patterns, through certain dishes, rituals and sensations: the smell of bonfires, the rustle of dry leaves, the first frost. Stir Up Sunday is around the corner, the last Sunday before Advent, when the prayer after Holy

Communion urges God to 'stir up the wills of your people'. It's generally taken as a cue to begin stirring, not our hearts, but mincemeat. Big bowls of raisins, currants, suet and brandy: Christmas puddings.

There's one dish I associate with this time of year that I learned on a road trip, visiting family in Switzerland. On the journey, we made a detour via Aosta in northern Italy, where we found a local trattoria on a side street near our hotel. Freshly covered in snow, the mountains all around leaned in over the ruins of a Roman theatre and handsome town houses. Inside the restaurant, it was warm and crowded. There was no menu. They just brought what they had that day. And what they had that day was risotto with cabbage and lard. It doesn't sound appealing, I know. But it was delicious, and I've been trying to recreate it ever since, never quite succeeding. A bit like keeping the heating off till Advent, my lard risotto tends to be a cause for complaint.

Our diversion to Aosta was, for me, an act of pilgrimage. Aosta is the birthplace of St Anselm (c.1033–1109), archbishop of Canterbury and the most brilliantly imaginative philosopher of his generation, if not of all the Middle Ages. Not only does he offer the Church an entirely new theory for how Christ's suffering and death atone for the sins of fallen humankind, but he also left the world what is still the most challenging and sophisticated philosophical argument for the existence of God.

Despite damaging rebuttals through the ages (most notably from Immanuel Kant), Anselm's Ontological Argument, as it's called, is crystalline. Neat and perfectly formed, it's the opposite of lard risotto, the philosophical equivalent of *nouvelle cuisine*. Requiring no authority from scripture, the barest version of the argument goes like this. Anselm asks us to entertain the notion that:

1. There exists that than which nothing greater can be conceived.
2. That than which nothing greater can be conceived exists either a) both in the imagination and in reality, or b) just in the imagination.
3. But it is greater to exist in both.
4. Therefore, on account of 1., that than which nothing greater can be conceived exists in both the imagination and in reality. Therefore, something than which nothing greater can be conceived exists in reality.

It may look like a trick, a joke even, but there has recently been a revival of interest in Anselm's argument, and various new versions have been published and discussed. A thousand years after its first formulation, Anselm's argument for the existence of God is still very much live. Perhaps *nouvelle cuisine* will have its day again too. (Although I rather hope not.)

What's often missed in discussions of the Ontological Argument is who it was written *for*. Anselm didn't come up with the argument for sceptical and secular-minded undergraduates (they didn't exist), but for monks under his care in the abbey at Bec in Normandy.

Look at the Ontological Argument again. Let's be honest, if you don't already believe God exists, Anselm's argument probably won't have you dashing into the nearest church or mosque or synagogue and falling on your knees.

The truth is, no philosophical argument will do that.

Anselm was writing and thinking within an Augustinian programme which starts with faith rather than ends with it. Augustine urged his readers to 'believe in order that you might understand'. Anselm adapted this into his motto: *fides quaerens intellectum*, faith seeks understanding. Not the other way round. Perhaps no one has come to faith through intellectual enquiry. Faith starts from the opposite of understanding, from foolishness, thank God.

> For the message about the cross is foolishness to those who are perishing, but to us who are being saved it is the power of God. For it is written,
>
> > 'I will destroy the wisdom of the wise,
> >     and the discernment of the discerning I will thwart.'
>
> Where is the one who is wise? Where is the scribe? Where is the debater of this age? Has not God made foolish the wisdom of the world?
>
> 1 Corinthians 1.18–20

Faith is less like the steps in a clever syllogism, and more like autumn: an enveloping context, a series of familiar sensations, more like a recipe than a reasoned argument. And you already have all the ingredients, including the lard, I hope.

.....

IN THE EAVES OF OUR COTTAGE a few years ago, I found an abandoned wasps' nest the size of a spacehopper.

In the beam of my torch, it looked like a ghostly Chinese lantern hanging from the rafters.

Recently I've watched wasps flying in and out of gaps under the cedar shingles in our roof again. Once or twice over the summer, I climbed a ladder to squirt toxic foam into the spaces where the shingles have lifted slightly in the heat. I even dangled out of a first-floor window for a better angle with the aerosol's nozzle, to no avail. The wasps kept coming and going, busier and buzzier than ever.

Now the queens have upped sticks, the drones no longer have to feed larvae in the nest. Fending for themselves and free to roam, they seem drawn to my study. I find myself frantically swatting at them during difficult phone calls with parishioners, or having to slide off camera during a church council meeting on Zoom in order to deal with a particularly persistent insect who takes delight in dive-bombing me through the prayers.

I can't help thinking the world would be a better place without wasps. You can tell me they're a crucial component in some corner of the ecosystem, but I say they've no place in the delicately balanced and threatened habitat of my study. I roll up this week's *Church Times* in readiness.

But then maybe being irritating, potentially dangerous, and aggressive is itself a reason for wasps' existence. Perhaps being a pain in the backside is a vital force in evolutionary dynamics. These days, oppositional and competitive algorithms (wasps, effectively) are introduced into machine learning systems: we have to think *against* something. All thinking, the AI programmers suggest, is inherently adversarial.

At crucial moments in the Bible, God acts in this way,

as an opponent, an obstacle, a vexation. The ultimate pain in the backside. Think of Jacob wrestling with the angel of the Lord till dawn (Genesis 32.24–31). Jacob cannot become Israel until he has faced this test and is able to walk away wounded.

And my pesky wasps are like the Pharisees in the gospel, always buzzing in with their tricky questions. It's an uncomfortable thought, but without the Pharisees and scribes and teachers of the law, there would be no gospel. Every story needs a baddie. Jesus has to be tested.

> A lawyer, asked him a question to test him. 'Teacher, which commandment in the law is the greatest?'
>
> Matthew 22.36

Jesus gives this lawyer a straight answer, essentially a swat: love God, love your neighbour. Next. Momentarily disarmed by the simplicity and directness of his response, the Pharisees are unprepared for Jesus' retaliatory question: 'What do you think of the Messiah? Whose son is he?' (Matthew 22.42). Jesus here resorts to a tactic he uses elsewhere: he turns the tables on his opponents and starts asking questions. In short, he knows how to be a wasp when the situation requires. It's a tactic liable to get you into trouble.

A few centuries before Jesus' falling foul of the law, Socrates, on trial for his life in Athens, described his own questioning of authority in these words:

> God has sent me to attack the city, as if it were a great and noble horse, to use a quaint simile, which was

rather sluggish from its size, and which needed to be
roused by a gadfly: and I think that I am the gadfly
that God has sent to the city to attack it; for I never
cease from settling upon you, as it were at every point
and rousing, and exhorting, and reproaching each
man of you all day long.

Socrates' questions and Jesus' questions are much more
dangerous than the questions of the Pharisees or the
Athenian authorities. While the Pharisees' questions pre-
suppose the laws and doctrines of this world, Jesus'
questions prompt us to be transformed by the renewing of
our minds (Romans 12.2). The Pharisees' questions are a
trap; Jesus' are a release.

We need wasps and gadflies. They show us that the real
dangers in our society do not come from the differences
between us, but the tug of tribalism and uniformity, the
cult of 'identity': the hive. The opposite of difference is not
sameness; it is indifference.

I must learn to put down the rolled-up newspaper and
put up with the wasps.

Gadfly God,
come to us as you came to Jacob,
and as Jesus came to Jerusalem:
unsettling and disruptive and unruly:
pester us into seeing beyond the tired and the stale,
needle us into new points of view,
harass us out of the hive of our habits,
and our hand-me-down identities:
inspire us to put on Jesus Christ,

your Son in whom we are uniquely ourselves,
and yet truly one.
AMEN

.....

DRIVE THROUGH A VILLAGE near here and a peculiar
sign catches your eye. It's the simplest sign imaginable. A
pole with a little board nailed up near the top on which is
written in capital letters the single word: LATIN.

Have I crossed some border? Are road signs here in
Latin? *Ite lente per vicum si placet.*

Actually, the sign is directing you to the home of
Martin, a friend and parishioner who works these days as a
Latin tutor. After years of teaching the language in
schools, Martin tells me, he's never for a moment fallen
out of love with Latin. He still goes dewy-eyed at the
mention of Virgil.

The other day I ran into Martin on the lane as I was
driving out of the village. Since contracting a hospital-ac-
quired infection a few years ago, Martin uses a mobility
scooter to get around. It was pouring with rain and Martin
was dressed for the weather in sou'wester and waterproof
trousers. I asked where on earth he was going on such a
miserable day. He told me he was travelling five or so miles
along the valley to a village where he knew there was a fish
van due.

'Kippers, Colin. I'm going for my kippers.'

And then, before we part, he asks after Theo who is now
studying Classics at university.

Most of Theo's classes are online, I tell him, but there's

one class each week that's always face to face: advanced Latin syntax.

Martin nods. 'With Latin syntax, you need to see the whites of their eyes.'

Latin is barely taught in our state schools these days. But Theo was lucky enough to attend a comprehensive where Latin is still offered and remains a popular choice at both GCSE and A Level. And yet, as a subject, it's always under threat; it is assumed to have no practical application in the world and is therefore of little use in the jobs' market. Apparently, employers aren't looking for lovers of Virgil. More fool them. And for this reason, some educationalists see Latin as a lost cause.

Perhaps I should've put a notice in the classified sections of today's newspapers – thanking the Latin teachers at Theo's school, thanking Martin, and also thanking St Jude. Because today is the Feast of St Jude, and St Jude is the patron saint of lost causes. You still come across notices in the classifieds thanking St Jude for prayers answered.

One of the twelve disciples, Jude inherited the lost causes portfolio on account of his name. Jude is shortened for Judas. Though in his gospel, John is at pains to point out that Jude is not to be mistaken for Judas Iscariot (14.22), the name 'Judas' was sufficiently tainted for Christians down the ages to avoid praying for this particular saint to intercede on their behalf. Hence, Jude became the last port of call, the saint to whom you turned only if truly desperate, if you felt no other saint would hear you or help you.

What do we think of Jude's lost causes? Not much. We admire winners. Attending the First World War centenary commemorations in 2018, Donald Trump chose not to visit the Aisne-Marne American Military Cemetery in northern France. 'Why should I go to that cemetery?' he asked. 'It's filled with losers' (Jeff Goldberg, *The Atlantic*, September 2020). Of course, Trump's right. But as we approach Remembrance Sunday, our hearts turn to these 'losers', those who lost or gave their lives that we might live in freedom.

We're in danger of forgetting a difficult but fundamental truth: at the heart of the Christian faith is a lost cause, a 'loser', a humble Galilean, a carpenter's son standing up to the combined authority of the Temple in Jerusalem and the Roman government, a peripatetic preacher and prophet who leads a ragtag of women, fishermen and tax collectors. This is a lost cause, surely?

It's certainly how it must have looked to Jude and the other disciples. Their messiah, their cause (in both senses of the word) is hung on a cross like a common criminal, with common criminals. His promises and signs have come to nothing, to failure.

That's how it looked to them. And Jesus says it himself:

'If the world hates you, be aware that it hated me before it hated you. If you belonged to the world, the world would love you as its own. Because you do not belong to the world, but I have chosen you out of the world – therefore the world hates you.'

John 15. 18–19

It follows, I think, that in a real sense, lost causes are the only causes worth having. Winning, success is *of the world*. It's to dance to the world's tune. The good news of Jesus

Christ is not dominion or wealth or triumph, it's not Christendom or even the Church; it is a narrow gate, and the road is hard (Matthew 7.14). It's a road that runs through a world built on licence rather than love, on greed rather than grace, on power rather than peace.

Truly, the only way to live is to be lost to the world. And to be lost is the only way to be found.

> *qui enim voluerit animam suam salvam facere perdet eam qui autem perdiderit animam suam propter me inveniet eam.*
>
> Matthew 16.25

You want a translation? Take a trip along the A338 until you see LATIN, and then ask for Martin.

.....

AT ALL SOULS' WE REMEMBER those we've loved and lost. And we've lost so many. At this evening's service, on a cold, windy November night, we listen to a recording of Keith Jarrett playing Gilbert and Sullivan's 'The Sun Whose Rays'. And people come up one by one out of the pews to light candles, and say prayers behind their masks. The space is filled with silent names.

Afterwards, I'm left alone in the empty church to tidy up. This evening's service is the last time we'll be gathering for worship before the next lockdown comes into force tomorrow. The key is turning on us again.

Now I'm snuffing out the candles and tipping away the trays of sand. With each candle snuffed, it gets darker and darker in the building. Until there are no lights at all, and I'm standing in the dark. Not for the first time this evening, I think of Maisie. Outside, the wind blows a gale through the churchyard and yet I can still hear bats fluttering about, high above my head in the rafters.

Unnerved, I fish out my mobile and turn on the torch. The polished brass eagle, brass candlesticks and organ pipes all leap and tumble towards me out of the darkness. I point the beam up at the roof, a lurching geometry of joists, rafters and arches.

I walk towards the altar, and think: I stood here, in front of this window back in March, and rescued two butterflies. Then, the window was filled with sunlight and colour. Tonight, the stained glass is a grid of blacks, dark blues and greys. As I move my phone back and forth, the shadow of the altar cross drifts and sweeps over the blankness of the window behind.

March feels a lifetime ago, and for some reason – perhaps it's the service we've just shared – I feel completely overcome. I pull off my mask, sit and pray in one of the choir stalls.

I know there are more and more cases of Covid in the villages. I know households where children are going hungry because work is drying up. I spoke to a couple this afternoon who run a restaurant in a nearby town. The woman wept as she told me she'd had to lay off all their staff. They're like family, she said. What will they do?

I don't know. What will any of us do?

Last week, Aggie's friend, Phoebe, found her neighbour lying on the pavement outside her house, unable to breathe. She knelt down and offered comfort and reassurance until an ambulance arrived.

As I walk towards the west door, the beam of my phone's torch sends shadows cowering under the pews and around the stone columns. I leave the church, locking up behind me. No butterflies this time, and the bitter east wind whips my cassock to my legs and blows the branches of the cedars about in the orange of the streetlights: a cold fire, comfortless.

.....

OUT OF THE VILLAGE, past the pond filling with leaves – vermilion, muddy golds and sulphur yellows; past the bedraggled ponies and up onto the top road. Another mile or so down the valley and into the next village. It was here, Emma remembers, that she used to come as a teenager to ring her Spanish boyfriend: it was the nearest payphone. Inside the kiosk was a phone with a dial, a telephone directory and a coin box, and an overpowering smell of cigarettes and urine. You'd have to love someone very much to stand in here for any length of time. She'd dial the international number, wait for the beeps when her boyfriend answered and then feed in the coins. A lot of coins, pockets' full, but at least it wouldn't show up on her parents' bill.

Emma is explaining the old routine to Aggie, who is fifteen and baffled. To Aggie, this all sounds Victorian or Neolithic, whichever's older. Aggie has her own phone always in her hand or her pocket, has myriad ways of communicating with her boyfriend whenever she wants – SMS, Snapchat, WhatsApp, *WhatEver*. Phones don't even have buttons these days, let alone dials. What's a dial?

And the phone box on the bend in the lane is long gone.

I remember when we'd have to take it in turns, watching football on the television, to stand with the aerial – just so – by the window. To move the aerial half an inch either way would result in our losing the signal, a fuzzy screen and a chorus of abuse from our friends on the sofa in front of the telly.

Now we live in a digital age. The WiFi is either working or it isn't. The screen is filled, or it's blank. It won't make any difference where you stand holding up a bit of bendy metal. Everything is ones and zeros. The phones in our pockets and the computers on our desks function in a binary universe. One or zero, open or closed, on or off.

In the same way, perhaps we're either blessed or not.

Blessed are the poor in spirit,
  for theirs is the kingdom of heaven.
Blessed are those who mourn,
  for they will be comforted.
Blessed are the meek, for they will inherit the earth.
Blessed are those who hunger and thirst
  for righteousness, for they will be filled.
Blessed are the merciful, for they will receive mercy.
Blessed are the pure in heart, for they will see God.
Blessed are the peacemakers,
  for they will be called children of God.
Blessed are those who are persecuted for
  righteousness' sake, for theirs is the kingdom of
heaven.

Matthew 5.3–10

These famous verses are known as the Beatitudes. They seem to be like buttons, a series of input/output functions. If you satisfy the conditions on the left of the 'for' (*hoti* in the Greek), then you will receive the rewards on the right: the kingdom of heaven, comfort, mercy and so on. For some, this is how religion works.

But religion doesn't work. Why would you ever suppose religion *works*? Does life work? Does love work? No, it fills you, changes you, changes the world around you, puts you to work.

What if, in the Beatitudes, Jesus offers us, not so much a series of buttons to press as a dial by means of which we can strive to attune ourselves?

For my children, tuning a radio means pressing a button or following a link. But for my father, listening to the test match on long summer car journeys, it meant twiddling a knob, moving a needle on a dial. It meant listening for the best signal. And every few miles, having to adjust again, trying to tune into the match by tuning out the static. Not on or off, but an endless process of finding, listening, losing, adjusting and finding again.

I think that's how we're called to read the Beatitudes: we are to be receivers, doing our best to tune into the message, twisting the dial of our lives towards mercy, peace and purity. Sometimes we have to tune ourselves through grief, persecution and despair in order to find the precious signal.

Pressing a button is easy. Fine-tuning the wireless takes skill, patience and practice. Deleuze talks of how 'Faith reflects upon itself and discovers by experiment that its condition can be given to it only as "recovered"'. Like Isaac to Abraham, faith's condition is given back, returned, recovered. You just have to keep listening and tuning.

The saint in the room is not the one who has pressed the button and reckons they've got the message coming through loud and clear, simple and sloganised. The saint in the room is the one holding the aerial for others, always watching, listening and adjusting themselves to recover a still, small voice coming through.

·····

IN THE FIFTEENTH CANTO of the *Inferno*, Dante describes his fellow Florentines as an ungrateful and malignant race. They are forged out of the mountain at Fiesole, he says, from which they descended, both literally and genealogically. The word Dante uses for the rock of which they're made is sometimes translated into English as 'granite' or 'flint'. But *macigno* refers specifically to a type of sandstone peculiar to the Upper Apennines. It's also called *pietra serena*, and its deep grey is visible throughout Florence, in the city's buildings and statuary.

The Florentines *are* their stone, Dante claims. Perhaps, like the Florentines, we all carry inside us something flinty, something of the hardness of the world.

I have a postcard above my desk of Donatello's *Saint George*. Now in the Bargello museum in Florence, the marble sculpture was commissioned by the guilds of the city to adorn their church, the Orsanmichele. As conceived by Donatello, George has a determined, defiant quality. Undaunted, head slightly turned, he's sizing up the dragon. Vasari describes him as expressing 'the beauty of youth, courage and valour in arms, and a terrible ardour'. With loosely curling hair over a clear brow, straight nose and strong jaw, he's the archetypal hero. Rock hard.

An actor friend of mine once described to me an encounter he had with his hero. He was working late one night, recording additional bits of dialogue for a film he was in. By the time he left the studio in Soho it was almost dawn and, before heading home, he thought: I'll stop for a quick coffee at Bar Italia on Frith Street.

The place was empty. He bought his coffee, sat down and was about to take a first sip when the street door opened, and in walked David Bowie.

It was just the two of them in this small bar at five o' clock in the morning. I asked my friend, 'What did you do?' He leaned in close, told me how Bowie ordered a coffee, lit a cigarette, but didn't sit down. Stood at the bar. There was a car waiting for him outside. Engine running. So, I asked again, 'What did you *do*?' My friend replied, 'I downed my coffee, got up, and walked towards him…'

'And?'

'I breathed his air.'

'You did *what*?'

'I breathed his air. Was that wrong?'

These days we might accuse my friend of grievously flouting social distancing guidelines. But back then his actions were just… well, creepy.

I was reminded of my friend's story yesterday when I went with Joey and Theo to pick up some emergency food boxes to deliver round the parish from the boot of my filthy Ibiza. Heroic as Horlicks, my car is the opposite of *macigno*.

When we arrive at the Church Centre, our breath steaming in the cold air, Glenda, the parish administrator, is still packing up bags and boxes. We come into the room, stamping warmth back into our toes, and stand back. Although Glenda is a hero, we don't want to breathe her air, or make her breathe ours.

Bowie was my friend's hero. Heroes must have many qualities, I suppose. But the most important is surely that we don't know them. When we get to know them, when Bowie turns and says, Hey, Alastair, what a lovely surprise, how're you doing? Sit down. Cigarette? then he's no longer your hero, he's your mate.

There's a story I heard once about a young Jewish boy who had learned the whole psalter by heart. From an early age, he could recite the psalms perfectly, parrot fashion, for his parents' friends at social gatherings. Almost perfectly. He'd slightly misheard (and therefore mis-learned) the penultimate verse of Psalm 23. Instead of saying: 'Surely, goodness and mercy shall follow me all the days of my life', he always gave the line as: 'Surely, good Mrs Murphy shall follow me all the days of my life'. It's funny, of course, but more than that: I think the child is right. Goodness and mercy are grand, abstract principles. Hero words. Hero ideas. We might want to breathe their air, but we wouldn't dare sit down and talk to them or call them our friends.

Good Mrs Murphy, on the other hand, we know her. She's the one packing up food boxes right now in front of me and the boys. She's the one calling her neighbours to check they're all right. She's dropping meals round to people who need a bit of extra care and love. She's buying Advent calendars for the kids in the village she knows come from households where the money won't stretch to luxuries like that. She's everywhere, been following us all the days of our lives.

A heart of flesh, not of stone.

Talking about goodness and mercy tells us something about God. But good Mrs Murphy, she shows us something about God, how God acts in the world and how we are called to act. For Christians, God lives with us, a God 'that we could hear, see with our eyes, look at, and touch with our hands' (1 John 1.1). As a result, for Christians, God is not ultimately understood or recognised as unattainable, unreachable, unaddressable, like one of our heroes. But as a person, frail and vulnerable among the frail and vulnerable.

What do heroes look like? Donatello's *Saint George*: shield, armour, sword, manly profile? Spare us. Look for heroes in church centres and parish rooms around the country; driving buses, sowing crops, delivering mail. Look for heroes working at the bedsides in our hospitals.

·····

THE FALL OF MAN was an historical event. It took place on the evening of Sunday, 6th October 2002. Still holding the incriminating apple, Adam fell and smashed to smithereens on the floor of the Metropolitan Museum in New York City.

Carved a couple of generations after Donatello's *St George*, Tullio Lombardo's *Adam* was created in Venice for the tomb of the doge Andrea Vendramin in the early 1490s. It is the first example of a monumental nude sculpture since the classical period. The languid *contrapposto* of Lombardo's *Adam* suggests not relaxation but reticence, a tacit, bolshy acknowledgement of wrongdoing: Adam here is literally (and metaphorically) on the back foot. Chin lifted, is he hearing God's calling to him in the garden? Or is that an expression of pride, that love of personal pre-eminence that Augustine recognises as the root of all sin, the cause of the Fall? Adam's lips are parted: perhaps he's preparing to admit he's afraid? Or to offer excuses? It's all her fault. Despite the calmness and serenity of the figure, there's regret in that face too, I think, a dawning and a dimming at the same time. As though he knows what's coming.

And now there he is, lying on the floor of the Met in twenty-eight large pieces and thousands of tiny fragments.

Before anyone could touch anything, or approach with a disastrous dustpan and brush, the conservators drew a grid on the floor of the room. And in each of the grid's squares they plotted the exact landing place of each tiny fragment. You couldn't ask for a better illustration of the doctrine of the Fall itself: from Adam to atom. We are broken away from the perfect whole, scattered across the floor, individu-ated, 'adamised', each in our own tiny, plotted square.

In his work on the Trinity, Augustine writes – in his Neoplatonic mode – of the soul, 'Loving its own power, and sliding away from the whole which is common to all into the part which is its own private property.' This is the Fall of Man, a sliding away from wholeness to fragmenta-tion. It's so easy. As G.K. Chesterton says, 'It is always simple to fall; there are an infinity of angles at which one falls, only one at which one stands.'

Using three-dimensional imaging technology to scan the marble pieces, conservators turned *Adam* into a jigsaw puzzle of immense complexity. You can watch on YouTube a film of how they slowly, painstakingly, over years, put him back together. It's a humpty-dumpty exercise of ingenuity and love: to make Adam good as new. But 'good as new' presents us with a dilemma. Adam *is* the Fall. To put him back together is therefore to undo him. In his perfect state he is imperfection personified. Shattered on the floor of the Met he is complete.

In his Second Letter, Brother Lawrence describes how he comes into the presence of God.

> I consider myself as a stone before a carver, whereof he is to make a statue: presenting myself thus before GOD, I desire Him to make His perfect image in my soul, and render me entirely like Himself.

Ultimately, Christians are not conservators; nor sculptors; they are (like Dante's Florentines) stone. We don't make ourselves, or make ourselves righteous; we're not authors of our own salvation. Rather than trying to undo the Fall by reassembling Adam, Christians live the resurrection by putting themselves, broken, in Christ.

Sovereign God,
may we who fall in Adam,
rise in Christ.

Broken in Adam,
whole in Christ.

Lost in Adam,
found in Christ.
AMEN

.....

REMEMBRANCE SUNDAY, and I'm driving over the hill
to the next village. It's early and the air is murky and
motionless, the lanes treacherous with wet leaves and jay-
walking pheasants. Coveys of partridges lift and glide in
front of me, like outriders. As I come across the brow, the
view widens, blank, and I pull over. Climbing out of the
Ibiza in my cassock, I go and stand at the barbed wire
fence overlooking the valley invisible in the mist below.
The solid rucks and folds of the downs grade away into an
enveloping featurelessness.

In the damp, still air, each barb of each cluster of barbs
along the whole twisted line of fence is tipped with a drop
of water. Weeping wire. And, truth be told, I feel like
weeping myself this morning. The Act of Remembrance
I'm about to take is – to all intents and purposes – against
the law.

On instructions from the government, I am actively to
discourage people from attending a service at which we
pay our respects to those who gave their lives for our
freedom and safety. The government guidance for Acts of
Remembrance goes on: 'Members of the public are
legally permitted to stop and watch the event as spectators'. No one – *but no one* – is ever a spectator at any act
of worship. The people hoping to attend this morning at
the war memorial are not coming to spectate. This isn't a

darts match or a Punch and Judy show.

But then it occurs to me, perhaps we should take pride in seeing ourselves as spectators. After all, spectators are above the fray. It's for them that gladiators gladiate and players play. Spectators buy the tickets; and who pays the piper calls the tune. The Ancient Greeks thought of their gods as 'watchers', spectators enjoying a long-running soap opera called *Homo sapiens*. In the theatre, the highest tier of seating is 'the gods'. The German philosopher, Martin Heidegger (1889–1976), even suggests the word for God, *Theos*, derives from the Greek word *theaomai* – I watch, I behold. It's a pretty idea, but false, etymologically speaking. Even so, in English, our word 'divine' can mean 'of God' or godlike but is also a verb meaning to search out or discover or see. And in an obscure corner of his voluminous argument against Eunomius, Gregory of Nyssa also argues that the *name* of God suggests oversight and foresight.*

But even if the Greeks thought of their gods as watchers, we definitely don't. For Christians, whenever two or three are gathered in his name, Christ is *among* them (Matthew 18.20); He is *in* the world, even if the world does not recognise him (John 1.10); He is *with* us always, to the end of the age (Matthew 28.20). God is no more a spectator than we are. Not watching us, but here, in the fray, with us; God has skin in the game.

> 'So do not fear, for I am with you;
>   do not be dismayed, for I am your God.
> I will strengthen you and help you;

---

* See Gregory of Nyssa, *Contra Eunomium XII, Patrologiae Cursus Completus, series graeca* (Paris: Migne, 1857–1886) vol.45:888D.

I will uphold you with my righteous right hand.'
Isaiah 41.10

Driving down into the mist, winding through the eerily locked-down village, I'm surprised by the number of people out walking their dogs this Sunday morning wearing medals on their overcoats, all heading in the direction of the war memorial. By the time I reach the memorial myself, the churchyard is full of people waiting quietly, not a spectator among them.

In the silence, we stand together, lots of us – two metres apart – and remember. Every year at this time, I remember my father's great-uncle Bobby. In my parents' dining room, there's a portrait of Uncle Bobby as a little boy.

During the Battle of Jutland in May 1916, Bobby was serving as a sub-lieutenant on HMS *Queen Mary*, a fast and lightly-armoured battlecruiser. That morning, the British battlecruisers bore the brunt of the German shelling. Built for speed and manoeuvrability, the battlecruisers' light armour made them particularly vulnerable. Taking a direct hit to its magazine, the *Queen Mary* exploded, split in two, and sank in seconds.

Bobby survived the explosion, and found himself in the water, relatively uninjured. He had even managed to grab a life jacket. Hours later, survivors from the *Queen Mary* were picked up by a German destroyer. Bobby was not among them. Weeks later, one survivor wrote to Bobby's father from a German prisoner-of-war camp to say how they had become desperately cold in the water and were almost overcome by the thick clouds of oil fumes. Bobby had offered this man his life jacket, 'for which action I shall never forget him, although I had only known him a few days'.

Just eighteen of HMS *Queen Mary's* crew of one thousand two hundred and sixty-four men lived. A friend later described Bobby as the 'soul of honour and chivalry'. Bobby's body, along with many others, was washed up on the coast of Norway. He was identified by the ring he was wearing which bore his initials – AWP (Bobby was a nickname). His mother never recovered from the loss. My aunt keeps that ring safe. And a few years ago, at the centenary commemorations for the Battle of Jutland held on the Orkneys, Joey read the lines from Binyon's poem: 'They shall grow not old...' in front of presidents and prime ministers. Under his shirt and tie, he was wearing Bobby's ring on a chain around his neck.

We will remember them, even as we are remembered by God, who is not watching us, spectating, but with us in the clouds and darkness, loving, and weeping too probably.

.....

IF YOU WERE GOING TO CLAIM a connection with a character in the Bible, you'd probably choose someone heroic or wise or righteous. Moses, say. Or someone flawed but inspired, like David or Paul. I have a connection with a character in the Bible. It's not a real connection, of course. I can't claim lineage or anything like that. But I share a name, a relatively unusual name, and it always leaps out at me when this obscure passage very occasionally crops up.

Now Sisera had fled away on foot to the tent of Jael

wife of Heber the Kenite; for there was peace between King Jabin of Hazor and the clan of Heber the Kenite. Jael came out to meet Sisera, and said to him, 'Turn aside, my lord, turn aside to me; have no fear.' So he turned aside to her into the tent, and she covered him with a rug. Then he said to her, 'Please give me a little water to drink; for I am thirsty.' So she opened a skin of milk and gave him a drink and covered him. He said to her, 'Stand at the entrance of the tent, and if anybody comes and asks you, "Is anyone here?" say, "No."' But Jael wife of Heber took a tent-peg, and took a hammer in her hand, and went softly to him and drove the peg into his temple, until it went down into the ground.

Judges 4.17–21

Grim. And let's face it, Heber the Kenite isn't a character you'd choose. I mean, he doesn't even do the deed. He's only mentioned because he's married to the murderer.

I've been suffering recently from what you might call 'Sisera's Revenge'. This Heber has been waking every morning with a headache that feels as if Jael has hammered his skull to the headboard. Nothing budges the pain except cans of cold Coca-Cola and hot showers. Ideally at the same time. And paracetamol. All unavailable to poor Sisera. Mind you, with a tent peg through your temple, paracetamol probably wouldn't do a lot of good.

I take to haunting the house in my dressing gown and lockdown beard, crouching by the fire or heating up chicken soup on the stove, or sitting half-heartedly at my desk, cradling my head. I'm sure it's not Covid, just congested sinuses. Whatever the cause, it's led me to do some thinking about pain.

There's a lot of pain in Christianity. Today is the Feast of Christ the King, a day on which we picture a pain-free Christ seated in majesty on a throne, holding the symbols of kingship, risen and far removed from 'the headache (*sic*) and the thousand natural shocks / That flesh is heir to'. Or so we're led to think.

In cell seven of the Dominican convent of San Marco in Florence, Fra Angelico (1395–1455) painted Christ the King in traditional mode, seated in majesty, with the orb and sceptre. But he's not wearing a kingly robe here; he's dressed in a simple white tunic. And he's blindfolded. His crown? Thorns. Stranger still, a disembodied face spits at him; we can see the flying spittle. And he's surrounded by hands. One hand lifts a cap in sarcastic salute. Another slaps him. Another beats him around the head with a stick.

Fra Angelico has painted a unique (as far as I know) conflation of Christ the King and the Mocking of Christ, a Pantocrator in pain. While he is mocked as 'King of the Jews', the King of Creation is seated in majesty. And the mocking itself is not given in Ribera-style grisly (and gristly) detail; this is not a naturalistic rendering of the mocking of Christ, but a schema. For the purpose of devotion, Fra Angelico analyses the scene down to its atomic components. What he offers is a depiction of pain itself. In other representations of Christ's passion, we're caught up in the drama, our emotions engaged, we're moved to pity. But here, there's just the raw reality of pain. Not who's doing it to whom or why and when: just gob, hands, sticks.

Here's your Christ, your king. In pain.

To meditate on the sufferings of Christ like this is not medieval or ghoulish, as is sometimes suggested. To think so is to push pain away, to banish it, to stand in the shower with a Coca-Cola waiting for the paracetamol to kick in.

Simone Weil suffered excruciating headaches all of her short life. She wrote this:

> Each time that we have some pain to go through, we can say to ourselves quite truly that it is the universe, the order and beauty of the world, and the obedience of creation to God that are entering our body. After that, how can we fail to bless with the tenderest gratitude the Love that sends us this gift?

Honestly, I don't have Weil's courage and strength. Few do. I can't manage to see pain as a gift or blessing or cause for thanksgiving. I venture it's not a gift any of us like to receive. But Weil also says, 'Suffering is to joy what hunger is to food.' Suffering's end, suffering's satisfaction – is joy. But it's worth noting that Weil doesn't say 'suffering is to joy what hunger is to *satiety*'. Suffering and hunger belong to us. But joy, like food, remains outside of our control; it must be given, and received.

I appreciate waking the next day, not to a hammering head and rain outside, but to this gift of a cloudless late autumn day and a sense – despite everything – of freedom. I walk to the top of the hill, and thank God.

. . . . .

CRESCENTS OF ASH AND DIRT under my fingernails; I've

been lighting a fire in the study to keep warm. Apart from my resorting to safety matches, these are actions with which even my distant, hairier ancestors would've been intimately familiar.

Now my grubby fingers are tapping in the login details for a Zoom meeting on my laptop. Faces of colleagues and friends pop up out of the 'waiting room' onto a screen of liquid crystal and we begin chatting. To my ancestors – even their less hairy descendants – this would be fantasy, a spell. Like the wicked queen's enchanted mirror, mirror on the wall, this screen talks to me.

That my monkey hands can light fires and touch-type is extraordinary. But we're liable to let our brilliance blind us to a buried assumption here. I talk about going from hearth to laptop, from the primordial to the present, as though I were progressing from one to the other. But I'm in danger of forgetting that when the Zoom meeting is over, I'll return to the logs and bellows, that I can still feel the cold. How much have we really changed?

And even during the Zoom meeting, I'm still – somewhere deep down – prone to all the habits, reflexes and prejudices of my ancestors. I look at these faces on the screen – as my ancestors must've done around the fire – with curiosity. I can't help appraising them, not consciously judging, but assessing according to ancient, ingrained criteria. I notice his tired eyes behind specs, her uncombed hair. Is that a glass of wine? Bit early, isn't it?

And in the backgrounds, behind people's heads, I start to pick out little clues and markers that subtly impinge: he has model aeroplanes on the sideboard behind him; the bishop has polished guitars mounted on his study wall; she has posh-looking invitations arranged – a little ostentatiously? – on her mantelpiece. Michael's bookshelves are a chaotic but scholarly jumble of biblical commentaries and bursting box files.

Even when we're isolated from one another, even when we're confined to our own homes and communicating on a screen, human beings are – fundamentally – still sitting around the fire, fascinated by each other. We live in and through a complex web of shared social signs and signals. Just as we regard others, they surely regard us, judge us, appraise us. Is Colin picking his nose?

I share this regarding with other human beings, but not with the logs in the grate or with my stowaway cat lying spread out on the carpet in front of the fire. For Heidegger, it's this regarding that is the essence of our humanness, the fact that my being, existing here and now is an issue for me. I can light fires and handle video-conferencing software, but that doesn't make me human. What makes me human is the fact I regard myself as being a lighter of fires and attender of meetings. And in the process, I regard others and regard them regarding me, as you're doing now. We're embedded in a world of shared meaning.

Heidegger offers us a richly complex language for describing and questioning our being in the world. But at the heart of his thinking is a set of ideas that had already been given moral and dramatic expression in the Old Testament.

It happened, late one afternoon, when David rose from his couch and was walking about on the roof of the king's house, that he saw from the roof a woman bathing; the woman was very beautiful.

2 Samuel 11.2

That afternoon, David assumes he is unregarded. Bathsheba's husband is away in battle, so David, the king, summons her. Afterwards, when David has made her pregnant and orchestrated her husband's death, the prophet Nathan tells David a story. A rich man, he says, takes a poor man's lamb and has it slaughtered and served for his guests. David responds: 'The man who has done this deserves to die' (2 Samuel 12.5). Then Nathan turns to the king: 'You are the man!' (7). Nathan forces David to recognise himself, to regard his own actions, his own being, even as he is regarded by God. The prophet does not have a crystal ball, but a mirror.

Because we can manipulate the world to our advantage – lighting fires and looking into each other's houses through laptop cameras – we feel we're somehow outside the world, regarding unregarded. Like David on his rooftop, masters of all we survey. But:

'Nothing is covered up that will not be uncovered, and nothing secret that will not become known. Therefore whatever you have said in the dark will be heard in the light, and what you have whispered behind closed doors will be proclaimed from the housetops.'

Luke 12.2–3

To live truly and honestly, to live humanly, Jesus is saying, is to live in the light, out loud, and open to judgement.

We're encouraged these days to protect and value our privacy. Bathsheba's privacy is violated when David spies on her. But it's the privacy of David's vantage point (and status) that affords him the opportunity to spy on her in the first place. Privacy is not an unconditional good.

After this dreadful year, one of the things we long for most is the opposite of privacy: to be in the light, together with one another. Perhaps it's not our privacy that needs protecting so much as our threatened, ancestral capacity for openness.

.....

ON MY WAY BACK FROM ST MICHAEL'S this evening, I stop at Emma's father's grave. It's dusk and the woods all around are full of the clatter and clamour of pheasants going up to roost.

The headstone in front of me: just a name and dates. And yet I know George is down there with a bottle of Poire Williams, the lethal eau de vie to which he was extremely partial. Grave goods.

At his funeral, George's coffin was carried by serving members of the SAS, the unit of which George had been a founding member. When the coffin was being lowered into the ground, one of the soldiers stepped forward, knelt down and spoke quietly into the grave, too quietly for me or any of us to make out the words. They were for George. It was one of the most moving moments I've ever witnessed at the graveside.

Afterwards, I asked the soldier what it was he'd said and he told me he'd recited a few lines of *The Golden Journey to*

*Samarkand* by James Elroy Flecker. 'We always say this one verse,' he said, 'over the body of any fallen comrade.'

> We are the Pilgrims, master; we shall go
> Always a little further; it may be
> Beyond that last blue mountain barred with snow
> Across that angry or that glimmering sea.

And after these words had been spoken, the soldiers poured in sand from Crete, where George had fought so bravely. Balls of steel.

I miss him.

Standing in the mist, a barn owl hooting in the beeches behind me, I feel the weight of loss, pressing. Last week I took three funerals in two days. These are small villages, and the hearse doesn't go unnoticed. On a cold, late-autumn afternoon, and to the rumbling of distant ordnance on Salisbury Plain, the undertaker walks slowly ahead of the cortege, off the High Street and towards the church.

> How long, O Lord? Will you forget me forever?
>  How long will you hide your face from me?
> How long must I bear pain in my soul,
>  and have sorrow in my heart all day long?
>
> Psalm 13.1–2

Always a little further.

# MUSIC

AT ALL SOULS' WE REMEMBER — PAGE 186
Keith Jarrett, piano, 'The Sun Whose Rays' by Arthur Sullivan and W.S.
Gilbert and Keith Jarrett, *La Fenice* (ECM, 2006)

OUT OF THE VILLAGE — PAGE 188
'Dimming of the Day / Dargai', Richard & Linda Thompson, *Pour Down Like Silver* (Island, 1975)

IN THE FIFTEENTH CANTO — PAGE 191
'The Mysteries', David Bowie, *The Buddha of Suburbia* (BMG International/EMI/Virgin, 1993)

THE FALL OF MAN — PAGE 194
'Misere', The Durutti Column, *Vini Reilly* (Factory, 1989)

REMEMBRANCE SUNDAY — PAGE 197
'Peace Piece', Bill Evans, *Everybody Digs Bill Evans* (Riverside, 1959)

IF YOU WERE GOING TO CLAIM — PAGE 200
'Passio', William Basinski, *Lamentations* (Temporary Residence Ltd, 2020)

CRESCENTS OF ASH AND DIRT — PAGE 203
Arvo Pärt, 'Spiegel im Spiegel', Papa M, guitar, *A Broke Moon Rises* (Drag City, 2018)

ON MY WAY BACK FROM ST MICHAEL'S — PAGE 207
'The Heavy Heart of Ando-Yeap', D. Charles Speer, *Arghiledes* (Thrill Jockey, 2011)

# WINTER

MARLBOROUGH HIGH STREET is handsome and broad. At chucking-out time on a Saturday night in the run-up to Christmas, the pavements are crowded, noisy and occasionally a bit punchy; bouncers are kept busy outside the Royal Oak; and the glowing ends of cigs and spliffs dance like will o' the wisps in dark corners of the supermarket car park and at the bus stop, or on Treacle Bolly, the obscurely named hill overlooking the town.

But I'm parked up, and the place is deserted. Fog billows in over the roofs. The pubs are shut, the roller grills in the kebab shops aren't rolling. Christmas lights blink and twinkle along the empty street: blue icicles and golden stars and nets of little bulbs hanging from the balcony of the red-brick town hall. The stubborn cheerfulness of the lights only heightens a general air of lockdown desolation.

Perhaps it's my mood, but sitting in the car with the heater on full and news on quietly, I can't help asking myself, what purpose do they serve, these lights and gewgaws? When there are no shoppers, no revellers, no brass bands, no carollers – why has the town gone to the effort of putting up all these lights and trees? What are they for?

The answer, I know, is that the lights, the decorations and traditions are for us all to mark and celebrate the birth of a Saviour. It's fine as an answer. I don't have a problem with the answer; it's the question – what are they for? – that bothers me, my own instinctive resorting to the language of purpose, function and utility.

The language of purpose has been with us a long time. From the start, I suppose. Speaking in a circle, the language of purpose is the purpose of language.

According to Aristotle, we can ask of anything why it is what it is. And there are, he argues, four answers. We can say what it's made of, what form it takes, what causes it, and finally, what it's *for*.

Look at any aspect of the universe – Christmas lights on a high street, for example, or indeed the high street itself, and we should be able to say what it's for. First published in 1779, David Hume's *Dialogues Concerning Natural Religion* comprises a series of discussions between fictional characters with conflicting views. One character, Cleanthes, argues that there's a 'curious, machinelike adapting of means to ends throughout all creation'. Cleanthes concludes that 'the Author of nature is somewhat similar to the mind of man, though possessed of much larger faculties'. He uses analogy, comparing the orderly functioning of human artefacts with the apparently orderly functioning of nature.

My Panasonic RC 80 alarm clock/radio from 1980 (still going strong) is *for* something and what it's for is evident in its design. Likewise (by analogy), the world displays the complexity and purposiveness of my alarm clock radio, so it must have been designed by someone with an end in mind. It's for something, right?

While I recognise the appeal of arguments like this, they're a bit like those coffee ones you get in a pack of Revels. Whether arguments for the existence of God from the appearance of design in the world work or not, you only ever end up with a Designer, an Author, as Cleanthes puts it, not the engaged, loving, troubling God of revelation. It's just a bit... meh. And you reach back into the bag, hoping for a toffee one, say, or a chocolate-coated raisin.

In Hume's *Dialogues*, Philo demolishes Cleanthes' arguments, or at least lands some bruising blows (before the bouncers are able to pull them apart). The argument from design, as it's often called, is far from impregnable, which brings me back to my original question: why am I thinking in terms of purpose or design at all? Why do the Marlborough lights have to be *for* anything?

What if putting up all these lights, bringing all these trees into our homes, fetching down decorations from the attic or the back of the cupboard is nothing to do with purpose? Could it be the case that it's the beautiful purposelessness of it all that points to God?

I'm talking about an argument for the existence of God from sheer, pointless joy. To the shepherds outside Bethlehem, the angel says: 'Do not be afraid; for see – I am bringing you good news of great joy for all the people' (Luke 2.10). No mention of purpose or function. Just joy. Jesus teaches his disciples not in order to impart knowledge, or to share arcane secrets about the workings of creation, but just for joy.

> 'I have said these things to you so that my joy may
> be in you, and that your joy may be complete.'
> John 15.11

Despite what advertisers tell us, we can't purchase joy, design for joy, or even have joy as a purpose. Joy is given.

Joy happens. Joy comes to us. Advent. It arrives.

Looking back up the locked-down high street, I realise I love the fact the lights are on, regardless of there being no one here to witness them but me. In the murk and the cold, they're there. Despite all the headlines and uncertainty, they're there. A light shining in the darkness. Don't ask what it's for; just walk towards it.

.....

A PASSAGE STRUCK ME from one of Bonhoeffer's letters recently. A German Lutheran theologian and pastor, Dietrich Bonhoeffer (1906–1945) was imprisoned by the Nazis for his resistance to the Reich. On 21st November 1943, he wrote to his student and friend Eberhard Bethge from Tegel prison on the outskirts of Berlin.

> A prison cell, in which one waits, hopes – and is completely dependent on the fact that the door of freedom has to be opened from the outside, is not a bad picture of Advent.

Like Bonhoeffer, who was executed in 1945, St Paul regularly found himself in trouble, and in custody. At Philippi, in what is now northern Greece, Paul was thrown into jail with his friend Silas. (A couple of millennia later, my bruised and battered brother-in-law, Johnny, was just a few cells down the corridor.)

> About midnight Paul and Silas were praying and singing hymns to God, and the prisoners were listen-

ing to them. Suddenly there was an earthquake, so violent that the foundations of the prison were shaken; and immediately all the doors were opened and everyone's chains were unfastened.

Acts 16.25–26

The door of freedom was opened, dramatically, from the outside. The guard assumes all his prisoners have escaped. After all, who wouldn't take this miraculous opportunity to get away? And that guard prepares to kill himself for shame. But 'Do not harm yourself,' says Paul from the darkness, 'for we are all here' (Acts 16.28). None of the prisoners have chosen to flee. Why not? Perhaps because, like Bonhoeffer, they've recognised a deep truth about confinement and isolation: the walls and the chains and the fetters and the rules and the law all make no difference whatsoever. In fact, they're a positive boon because they reveal how we're – all of us – always waiting, hoping, completely dependent on a door being opened from the outside.

We're all here.

. . . . .

IN THE DENTIST'S WAITING ROOM, I was disappointed to find no copies of *Men's Health* or *What Car?* to leaf through. What with my sinuses, toenails and the imminent (be honest, Colin) demise of the Ibiza, both publications would've been of mild interest to me for once. But all the magazines have been removed in compliance, I'm told, with safety guidelines. Oh well, I'll scroll through

Instagram instead, or glance at the headlines or browse Mauritian beachfront properties on Airbnb. I can dream, while away the waiting, waste the waiting.

A dentist's waiting room, a triage ward, a departure lounge, a railway platform: we set aside places and times for waiting. But actually, no sooner have we boarded the train than we're waiting for it to arrive, checking our watches against timetables. However successfully we manage to distract ourselves, waiting is something we do wherever we are and whether we like it or not – mainly not.

Of course, some of us are paid to wait, professionals. In *The Pickwick Papers*, Dickens notes how 'Waiters never walk or run. They have a peculiar and mysterious power of skimming out of rooms, which other mortals possess not'. And one of the most arresting and well-known images in all modern philosophical writing concerns just such a person:

> Let us consider this waiter in the café. His movement is quick and forward, a little too precise, a little too rapid. He comes toward the customers with a step a little too quick. He bends forward a little too eagerly; his voice, his eyes express an interest a little too solicitous for the order of the client. He tries to imitate in his walk the inflexible stiffness of some kind of automaton while carrying his tray with the recklessness of a tightrope walker. All his behaviour seems to us a game.

Writing in the early 1940s, Jean-Paul Sartre describes

this waiter as an example of bad faith: the man is playing at being a waiter, allowing himself to be subsumed into a role. His 'condition is wholly one of ceremony', Sartre says, a pretence; 'As if his whole vocation/Were endless imitation', as Wordsworth puts it. But aren't we confusing two distinct meanings of the word 'wait' here? There's a difference, surely, between waiting tables and waiting *per se*?

Julian of Norwich doesn't think so. She talks about waiting on God, and she recognises no distinction between waiting as serving and waiting as anticipating. She offers us a parable which begins like this:

> The lord sits in solemn state, in rest and in peace; the servant stands by respectfully in front of his lord, ready to do his lord's will. The lord sends the servant to a certain place to do his will. The servant does not just walk but suddenly springs forward and runs in great haste to do his lord's will out of love.

Waiting here is an attentive readiness. Julian's servant responds with the same alacrity as the waiters described by Dickens and Sartre, but there's no suggestion of bad faith, ceremony or automation. In Julian's parable, the servant acts 'out of love'. Julian asks us to consider waiting not as a role, a job or a function, something we assume, but as an essential aspect of our being human. For Julian's servant, waiting is akin to loving, an expression of loving.

I think we're all waiters. We can wait lovelessly, as Sartre suggests, out of duty or contractual obligation or in bad faith. We can waste the waiting, scrolling through Instagram. Or we can wait well, lovingly, deeply. To wait deeply isn't to pass empty time before a train arrives. Nor is it a series of assumed, rote actions and gestures. Waiting well is an attunement of ourselves to the will of God. Waiting is the quiver that runs through all things, the glorious incompleteness that longs to be completed, a sort of excitement at the heart of creation. Like the cosmic background radiation pervading the whole universe, waiting is the key in which creation is written.

To be fully alive, Mother Julian suggests, is to wait, to attend, to be on the edge of your seat all the time.

The dentist will see you now.

.....

FREEZING FOG, and overnight all the cow parsley seed heads are turned to silver brooches, cobwebs to lace, and the old man's beard and briars in the hedgerows to tangles of icy filigree. If the sun were to come out, diamonds would spill everywhere. The weather has made of my garden a duchess's dressing table.

Baffled pigeons peck at ice in the rusty water butt by the greenhouse where they're used to drinking. I try to break the ice for them with my elbow, but the ice is solid. Flints and kettles of hot water are useless. Even at midday there's no sign of the fog lifting; it drifts through the branches of dead ash trees and greys out the yews in the churchyard. At dusk, from the ridge of the down, headlights on the top road blaze briefly out of the wintry murk, and are snuffed moments later.

Under the muffling fog it feels as though the world has stopped, or disappeared altogether. After a few days of this, it's easy to imagine the landscape itself has shrunk to a few metres round. We're all suddenly solipsists: the weather (as well as the virus) has forced us back into self-isolation.

And yet there's something I love about these conditions. It is weather-in-waiting, perfect for the season. After all, Advent is the year's waiting room. We're waiting for the fog to lift, the ice to melt. For light to shine in the darkness, for a vaccine, a saviour.

I'm still fussing over that distinction between waiting well and waiting poorly, wasting the wait. To wait well is to be patient, I suppose. Fairly obvious, and a little nanny-ish. But it seems to me there's more to patience than 'Rome wasn't built in a day'. The word 'patience' has its root in the Latin *patior* – I suffer. So, to wait is to suffer; it is to be at the mercy of the world. We cannot bend the world entirely to our will; instead, we must be patient, endure its whims, and its waiting rooms.

In that passage from his first letter to the Corinthians, where Paul describes love as patient, I don't think he means to say love requires a preparedness to put up with a partner's peccadilloes; he's not saying love is tolerant. He is saying love is *long-suffering*.

At a funeral this morning, I watched a widow throw a single cut rose into the cold ground after her husband of forty-five years. She suffers because she loves. Love is patient in precisely that sense.

In his book *The Stature of Waiting*, Anglican priest W. H. Vanstone (1923–1999) talks about how,

> In authentic loving there is no control of the other who is loved: that he or she will receive is beyond the

power of love to ordain or know. So when our work of love is done we are destined to wait upon the outcome. By our activity of loving we destine ourselves, in the end, to waiting.

When we wait for someone or something, the outcome matters to us, and that outcome is in the hands of someone else, in the gift of someone else. It's here, Vanstone says, that waiting becomes divine.

God so loved the world that he gave his only Son (John 3.16), and his Son comes not to be served but to serve (Matthew 20.28; Mark 10.44), to wait on the world. The waiting incorporates service, suffering and sacrifice. The Incarnation is, fundamentally, an act of waiting.

Having given final instructions to his disciples, and knowing he is on the point of being betrayed into the hands of the authorities, Jesus waits. He takes his disciples across the Kidron Valley to the Garden at Gethsemane. And the waiting is agony. He sweats blood (Luke 22.44). Vanstone again:

> Waiting can be the most intense and poignant of all human experiences – the experience which, above all others, strips us of affectation and self-deception and reveals to us the reality of our needs, our values and ourselves.

Jesus prays that, if it were possible, the hour might pass from him, 'yet, not what I want, but what you want' (Mark 14.36). The coming into alignment of his will with the Father's is the essence of waiting. Waiting empties us, makes room, offers our capacity for the longed-for other, for grace.

Vanstone talks about waiting as 'the activity of loving' but I think loving is just as much a passivity, a passion. It seems to me that to wait like this, like Jesus, is to be passive (another word deriving from *patior*) in the true sense: to suffer, to yield lovingly to the will of the other who matters.

It's during that hour of waiting, that hour in the garden, that Jesus Christ is revealed as fully human, and fully divine. When the arresting officers ask three times if he is Jesus of Nazareth, he answers three times 'I am he'. The repetition is deliberate. John's gospel is said to be structured around seven 'I am' sayings. Jesus says, I am the Bread of Life (6.35), the Light of the World (8.12), the Gate for the sheep (10.7), the Good Shepherd (10.11), the Resurrection and the Life (11.25), the Way, the Truth and the Life (14.6), the True Vine (15.1). But actually there are *eight* 'I am' sayings. And this is the last and greatest of them all, the culmination: I AM HE. At this moment, using God's name, I AM (Exodus 3.14), Jesus identifies himself with the Father. This is the beloved, the one who waits.

.....

EVERY YEAR WE FETCH DOWN a bag of Christmas decorations from the dark and mousey roof space, all packed carefully away last January. I say mousey, but it's less so since the squatter's arrival. Our rodent population has plummeted and I haven't had to resort to my clear plastic traps for months. Normally, the walls and ceilings of the cottage are full of fidgety skittering and pattering; out of the corner of your eye, movement along the skirting, a suspicious spill of lentils in the kitchen cupboard. All no more.

We open the bag of decorations together, reverently almost, fondly picking out favourites. There's a painted wooden St Nicholas I brought back from a monastery on Mount Athos. And various objects made by Joey, Theo and Aggie when they were at playgroups and primary school: knitted puddings, doughy stars covered in glitter, cut-out shepherds, angels and gingerbread men. There are even decorations – garish 70s baubles – that Emma and I have inherited, somehow, from Christmases of our own childhoods.

We inherit our faith too, or our lack of it. We carry it in our blood. But can that be right? Shouldn't our faith come to us in a Saul/Paul-style conversion experience on our own personal road to Damascus? Surely our faith must be ours, not handed down to us like Christmas decorations, or Granny's blue eyes?

I might have inherited my grandmother's blue eyes, or the family nose; but the point is they're *my* eyes, it's *my* nose. All the more so because I know where they've come from. Actually, I think a long-established, rooted, inherited faith might be just what we're looking for at the moment, approaching a Christmas that promises to be like no other in our lifetimes.

(I'm talking here about how we inherit religious faith, but of course atheism is just as heritable. Our political convictions and personal tastes all have, I suspect, dustier, older sources than we sometimes like to think. All our opinions and judgements have a whiff of naphthalene about them.)

At times of crisis we naturally turn to what makes us feel safe and secure; we yearn for warm, pebble-smooth familiarity. The ground-breaking, the fresh, the original can suddenly seem shallow, ephemeral and thin.

On social media during the early days of the first lockdown, people asked friends to share their top ten favourite albums, the films and books that have influenced them, photographs of themselves as children or as teenagers. And now, at Christmas, even when we can't go inside them, our ancient or not so ancient churches sit like magnetic north in the middle of our villages, towns and cities.

I think we should embrace this idea of inheritance. Of course, I recognise there's an opposing view. Something that's inherited, received, has overtones of indoctrination, or thoughtless, empty habit. This is W.H. Vanstone again, writing in 1977:

> The Church is an activity and product of freedom.
> We must exclude from the Church everything which,
> though 'religious' in form, is not the activity or
> product of freedom.

Vanstone's strict 'must exclude' is clearly a curtailment of the very freedom he's trying to advocate. Aside from this muddle, Vanstone's argument for radical freedom is also worryingly unscriptural: 'So then, brethren, stand firm and hold to the traditions which you were taught' (2 Thessalonians 2.15; see also 2 Thessalonians 3.6). And Paul's injunction to stand within the traditions we've inherited and learned is only a wise echo of what we hear in the Psalms over and over again. In Psalm 78, for example, the

Lord commands our ancestors to teach their children so that the next generation might know of God's deeds, might and wonders. 'Rise up and tell them to your children, so they should set their hope in God' (Psalm 78.5–7; see also Psalm 22.30–31).

I hand the bag of tinsel and baubles, the bunting and the crib set down from the attic and into Aggie's upstretched arms.

A hand-me-down faith can easily become, as Vanstone recognises, atavistic and dry, an enforced set of rote rituals. But it needn't. We can be as free and faithful in the traditions we inherit as we are in the expressions of worship and religious life we like to think of as chosen by us, as new or fresh or innovative. When Ludwig Wittgenstein (1889–1951) declares in *Culture and Value* that 'Ritual is permissible only to the extent that it is as genuine as a kiss', he strikes me as being more generous, and actually more Anglican than Rev'd Vanstone.

At my son Joey's confirmation (a ritual that encodes and passes on the doctrines and traditions of our faith), my parents gave him my grandfather's Bible. Tucked into the pages of Joey's great-grandfather's Bible are prayer cards, orders of service from funerals and baptisms, dried flowers, palm crosses and Christmas cards, all gathered over several generations. It is an embodiment of that precious plumb line of faith dropping down and rising up through centuries of Church, parish and family history. Questions of freedom or constraint or freshness do not arise, or shouldn't.

Also between the pages of this Bible is a letter to my grandfather written by his mother (the sister of Bobby who was killed at the Battle of Jutland) from her deathbed.

She writes to tell my grandfather he's been a wonderful, 'dearest son'.

> Thank you for all your love to me, she says. I feel I
> shall always be near you, and remember the veil
> between us is very thin – and we shall meet again.

The loving son who kept that letter in his Bible leaves that Bible to his son, who then gives it to my son at his confirmation. To me, this idea of handing on our faith, of that faith being given by the grace of God not in miraculous *moments*, but in *time,* long stretches of family time, parish time is a way of linking the past with the future, and us with eternity.

.....

BETWEEN THE HAMLET where I live and nearest village with a shop, a school and a post office, is a wooded ridge of downland known locally as the brail. One summer holiday back in the 1980s, my then teenaged brother-in-law, Johnny, worked on an archaeological dig up on the brail. A team from Indiana University was excavating the site of a Roman villa. On preliminary 'walks' across the area, they'd found *tesserae*, coins, roof tiles, buttons and glass medicine bottles. The findings from the subsequent dig were published a decade later by Indiana University Press. In the introduction to that book, the writers refer quaintly to 'village elders' who could recall how rubble from the villa was used in the building of roads in the middle of the twentieth century.

A few years ago, Nick bought a copy of the Indiana University book and a group of us went up onto the brail to try to find the site. Our children – young then – were expecting a romantic heap of marble columns, crumbling arches and rusting swords. They were disappointed by the undulating and soggy patch of clearing in the forest. It was a place we'd all walked past many times before without a second thought. But what disappointed the children fascinated the adults. How can something as massive and solid as a Roman villa just vanish? How can something as massive and solid as an empire decline and fall so as seemingly to leave no trace?

But then eight-year-old Maisie found something. A sort of tongue-sized and tongue-shaped terracotta fragment. We passed it between us. Could it be the rim of a bowl or jar? What particularly drew our attention was a clear thumb-print in the pottery.

If I asked you to remember the beginning of Matthew's gospel, you might recall the nativity story: 'Now the birth of Jesus the Messiah took place in this way. When his mother Mary had been engaged to Joseph...' But actually that's not the beginning of the gospel. That is verse eighteen. The first seventeen verses of Matthew's gospel are a family tree, sometimes called the stem of Jesse, tracing the lineage of Jesus back forty-two generations. Names crop up in the list that don't often get a mention: Jechoniah, Salathiel and Zerubbabel, for example. Remember them? I didn't think so. They're thumbprints, remnants, traces, all but effaced from history. (For the record – and I needed to look this up – all three were kings of Judah: 1 Chronicles 3.)

We leave out the first seventeen verses of Matthew's

gospel because we think they don't really matter. Instead, we cut to the chase: 'she was found to be with child from the Holy Spirit'. And we're off. It's hard to make a nativity play out of a family tree.

But Matthew's right; the thumb-prints are vital. The past is much closer than we think, and much more active in our lives. The Enlightenment's emphasis on the singular power of human reason unfettered by tradition, doctrine and established authority has left us somehow past-less, starting at verse eighteen, cut off from ourselves. The Enlightenment left us with museums.

Don't misunderstand me, I love museums. But they can make us feel we're only able to visit the past. Pay the entrance fee and you can have a poke about, peer into a few glass cabinets before going home. Matthew's point in opening his gospel with a genealogy is not that we can go back to the past, but that the past lives on in the present, in our veins. We are museums.

The first name on Matthew's list is Abraham. When God takes Abraham out of his tent and tells him to look up into the night sky, He says, "Look toward heaven and count the stars, if you are able to count them." Then he said to him, "So shall your descendants be"(Genesis 15.5). God goes on to describe a history of these descendants – slavery, freedom, a promised land – that has not yet happened. It's not so much a case of God knowing the future, more that there's no difference for God between future and past. The whole of creation is spread out before Him like the stars, like a living family tree, the Tree of Jesse with sap in. God sees it all: Roman villas being built and their ruins being used for roads. Eternal life doesn't mean living for ever, on and on; it means living on the stem now, in the story's unfolding.

When Maisie's find was taken to the museum in Devizes, they confirmed it was a section of Roman piping, part of a hypocaust heating system, they said. And so the thumbprint was certainly Roman.

In his dialogue the *Theaetetus*, Plato offers a model of how memory works. Socrates asks us to imagine that in the soul there's something like a block of wax. Our experiences press into this wax, make an impression and leave their mark on us. Socrates calls for us to make the wax in our souls 'deep and abundant and worked to the proper consistency'. His words remind us we should be yielding and soft, not hard and impervious. As for Socrates' wax, so for the potter's clay:

> We are the clay, and you are our potter;
> we are all the work of your hand.
> Isaiah 64.8

Handmade, we're all thumb printed all over.

.....

FOR THE FIRST TIME IN A FEW DAYS, the temperature nudges into positive territory. The world begins to drip and slide and flow. The beech trees crackle and shed ice from their crowns, dropping petticoats of crunchy snow around their boles.

I must've walked past this particular gravestone thousands of times. But it still moves me. And this afternoon, in the gloom, while I trudge back from St Michael's through the melting snow, I step off the path to pause. Mary's grave is in the far south-western corner of the churchyard, half-hidden under a scraggy yew, and towered over by a pair of sentinel beeches.

To the sound of dripping all around me, I read the familiar inscription:

Sacred
to the memory
of Mary Charlotte,
the beloved and only child of
Joshua and Jane Wright of
Newcastle-upon-Tyne.

For seven years the devoted Mistress
of Fosbury School.
She fell asleep in Jesus
September 5th 1856
Aged 26 years

Them also which sleep in Jesus,
will God bring with him. 1 Thess. iv, 14

A teacher at nineteen, so far from home. A village school, one big, noisy room, and Mary doing her best to drill the rudiments into boys destined to follow the plough, and girls to follow their mothers into service at the manor.

I imagine too, Joshua and Jane having to make the long journey south for the funeral. The way they specify on the inscription that Mary is their only child. 'Daughter' might have implied they had a son to console them in their loss. Mary is their only *child*. There's agony in that choice of word.

An unambitious example of Victorian gothic, the church at Fosbury, the next village down the valley from here, was completed in 1856, the year Mary died. I wonder if she insisted on being buried up here at St Michael's. Perhaps the brand-new churchyard at Fosbury had not yet been consecrated, or did it still seem depressingly empty, too lonely a prospect? During her seven-year tenure as school-mistress at Fosbury, Mary would've made the walk each Sunday to St Michael's. I see her wearing an unfashionable coal-scuttle bonnet, shawl over her shoulders, neatly darned here and there, prayerbook in hand, and a trail of pupils in the lane behind her. I imagine this is where she wanted to rest.

What were her seven years here like? An idyll? I doubt it. A feat of endurance? I'm not sure that's quite right either. 'Endurance' occurs in a passage of Paul's letter to the Romans that the bishop has been quoting a lot recently, to encourage us, I think, through lockdown. It goes like this:

> But we also boast in our sufferings, knowing that suffering produces endurance, and endurance produces character, and character produces hope, and hope does not disappoint us, because God's love has been poured into our hearts through the Holy Spirit that has been given to us.
>
> Romans 5.1–5

Personally, I don't find this encouraging at all. In fact, I've always struggled with these verses. The idea that suffering produces endurance smacks of the banal 'character-building' nonsense peddled at my public school, a rugger-mud-spattered cliché that derives ultimately from Nietzsche writing in 1888, the year he finally went mad: *'From life's school of war –*. What doesn't kill me makes me stronger'. The English public schools effectively turned Nietzsche's ugly 'life's school of war' into the even uglier 'schools for a life of war'. You need to be tough, to be strong, to endure, to win. Baleful nonsense. I wish I'd gone to Mary Charlotte's school instead.

So, what has the bishop seen in this passage that I'm missing? If we didn't know before, we've all learned what sufferings are this year. And endurance too. But the word in Greek that is translated as 'endurance' is *hupomonē*. *Hupomonē* literally means an 'under remaining'; it could be translated as 'patience'. It's related to words for abiding and dwelling. When Jesus tells his disciples that 'in my Father's house there are many dwelling places' (John 14.2), the word he uses for 'dwelling places' is *monai*, which is also the 'remaining' root of *hupomonē*. The word Paul uses in his letter to the Romans is more to do with *staying* than staying power. It is gentle and yielding, like wax, like clay.

And the word translated as 'character' in my version of Romans is, in Greek, *dokimen*, which means testedness, having been tested or proved or pressed.

So, Paul could be read as saying life's sufferings result in a determination to abide, to see it through. And this preparedness to stay leads to a proving of ourselves, giving rise in turn to a hope which is fulfilled in the pouring out of the Holy Spirit into our readied hearts. All this I understand.

Although words like endurance and character may sound as though they've been lifted from a public school prospectus or an army recruitment poster, Paul is actually advocating a yielding willingness, like soft clay, a preparedness to *abide*, and be *proved* or imprinted, qualities I imagine exemplified in Mary Charlotte. Her seven years at a village school in Victorian Wiltshire would've required deep wells of patience and love. Devotion indeed.

And He will bring them to abide, to remain, in His mansions for ever.

A prayer, before I leave, for Joshua and Jane.

.....

WOULD YOU ALL PLEASE stand for the bride.

And, on her father's arm, Natasha begins to walk up the aisle of St Michael's to 'Livin' on a Prayer' by Bon Jovi.

To be honest, if Natasha had asked for 'Too Drunk to F\*\*k' by the Dead Kennedys, I'd probably have said yes. I've known Natasha and her family many years. Her grandfather used to live in the old school house next door to us. His name was John Long but my children always called him 'Long Johns'. When John's wife, Ingrid, went into a care home, John would drive the few miles every day to be with her.

Ingrid used to run the raffle at the village fireworks, a highlight in the calendar. Before the huge bonfire was ceremonially lit, you'd hear a rumbling of the farm's articulated loader coming up the hill. And then the machine would emerge slowly from the darkness, it's lifting platform fully extended and jutting proud, high over the pile of wood, bales and farm detritus. John would be perched up there, magisterial, a big barrel of sump oil between his legs. The loader would come to a halt and John would raise some sort of blunt instrument, like a wrench, and hack off the barrel's bung, allowing dark oil to glug out over the flammable material below.

Then the fire would be lit.

In those days, Natasha helped Emma and me with the children. Now she runs popular peloton and line-dancing classes at the local leisure centre. Long Johns is long gone, and Ingrid too. They are much missed.

The groom, Luke, stands in front of me now, nervous and snatching glances back at Natasha as she comes up the aisle to meet him at the chancel steps.

The church is lit by candles and the lights from a huge Christmas tree. Natasha's father, head gardener down the road at the manor, has filled the church with greenery: twines of ivy round the columns and holly clustered with berries on the sills, and sprays of laurel.

Shadows hover in the corners, around the Saxon font, the rackety fuse board and rows of mouldering prayer-books. The air smells resinous and candley, and of John and Sylvia's homemade polish. Outside, guests are waiting, singing carols. We're only allowed fifteen masked people in the service.

Out of diligence, and just for the record, I did check Bon Jovi's lyrics. And I found they offered a compelling account of prayer. For those of you who may need reminding, the song tells the story of Tommy and Gina, who are struggling to survive on the salary Gina earns as a waitress in a diner while Tommy's union is out on strike. He has to pawn his guitar to make ends meet. Crying at night, Gina dreams of running away from it all. And yet they have each other, and that's enough.

Prayer doesn't make Tommy and Gina's life together any easier. There's no indication that their prayers are answered in any material way. Instead, prayer is how they live. They live on prayer. What does it mean to live on prayer?

While he's fasting in the desert, Jesus is tempted by the devil to turn stones into loaves of bread. Jesus answers his adversary with a quote from the Hebrew scriptures:

'One does not live by bread alone,
  but by every word that comes from the mouth of God.'
                                          Matthew 4.4

I suppose Jesus means living on prayer. I may not have bread, he's saying, but bread doesn't keep me alive anyway; God keeps me alive. You might say, that's all very well if you're not actually hungry. If you're hungry, you need bread. You don't tell a starving person just to pray harder; you feed them.

I think it's the needing that counts, knowing that we need. Hungry or satisfied, I live in need. To live in need is to live like Tommy and Gina: incomplete. It's to live in the knowledge that we're never *there*, only ever halfway there. And we can't get there under our own steam. It's actually a perfect message to hear at a marriage when a couple's need for one another is being sanctified in the vows they make before God.

In the gospels, Jesus comes to the poor, the sick, the forgotten, the blind and the broken not, I think, because he prefers them, or favours them. He comes to them because they need him. Because they live on prayer. 'Whatever you ask for in prayer, believe that you have received it, and it will be yours' (Mark 11.24). This isn't a spell or a superpower. Actually, it's a call for us to live in super-weakness, by faith, by believing, needing, asking, placing ourselves in dependence on God, like Jesus in the desert.

Live like this, and we'll make it, I swear.

.....

ABOUT A HUNDRED METRES into the tunnel, darkness envelops you. Without head torches or mobile phones, the only light is a tiny white pearl nearly half a kilometre ahead. Or is it dancing in front of your nose? It's impossible to tell. The acoustics in here distort sounds too, so drips and splashes and coughs are unplaceable in the auditory field. A shout of encouragement from far away at the tunnel's mouth sounds as though it's being whispered in your ear.

The Bruce Tunnel runs for almost half a kilometre under one of the parishes where I work. In the early years of the nineteenth century, the first earl of Ailesbury (wisely, in my view) refused the cutting of a steep-sided canal through his family's Savernake estate, a royal hunting forest that once stretched for many hundreds of square miles. Instead, the earl funded the digging of a tunnel under the forest. Opened in 1810, the Bruce Tunnel marks the summit of the Kennet and Avon Canal, which runs from Bath to Newbury.

A few years ago, I found myself playing 'designated adult', kayaking with Theo and his friend Matt through the tunnel. It's not an experience I'd choose to repeat, a bit like 2020. This year has felt like a long, dark tunnel. And right about now it's at its darkest: a new, more virulent strain of infection is abroad in our towns and villages. We sang carols unaccompanied on the village sports field the other day; unaccompanied because one of our beloved organists and her husband are sick with Covid, the other is vulnerable and shielding. There's chaos at the ports, still harsher restrictions on movement and freedom around the corner.

There's a point in the Bruce Tunnel when the light behind you has shrunk to a penny, and the light ahead appears not to be growing at all. Time dilates. And the darkness is stifling, substantial; it closes in. Or opens out into an unimaginable vastness, I can't tell which. Panic a heartbeat away.

And then Matt announces he's dropped his paddle. Deep breath, Colin.

Noses of our kayaks bumping against the invisible tunnel wall, we run our hands through the water. All our senses converge in our fingers. Though it oughtn't make any difference, we find it easier to search with our eyes closed. My fingers brush against mossy brick, weeds, mud and... finally – the handle of Matt's paddle. We resume our journey.

Whenever I hear that cliché, 'light at the end of the tunnel' – and we've heard it a lot recently – I think back to that hour in the Bruce Tunnel. I remember what it's like to have to work to keep fear in check, making steadily towards the circle of light, willing it to expand – button, golf ball, crumpet, planet – longing to emerge into it.

St John uses light and dark imagery throughout his gospel. At this dark time of year, many of us will have reflected on his Prologue:

> The light shines in the darkness, and the darkness did not overcome it. There was a man sent from God, whose name was John. He came as a witness to testify to the light, so that all might believe through him. He himself was not the light, but he came to testify to the light. The true light, which enlightens everyone, was coming into the world.
>
> John 1.5–9

This year we haven't heard the Christmas story; we've lived it. We are the people who have walked in deep darkness (Isaiah 9.2). The decree sent out by a distant power for everyone to be registered (Luke 2.1–5) sounds suspiciously like Track and Trace. An enforced journey through Roman-occupied Judea resembles a last-minute dash home through a Britain about to go into lockdown. And surely, Mary's pregnancy is 'an underlying health condition'? She's one of the vulnerable who have been so at risk this year. With Joseph and Mary, we've all been looking for light at the end of the tunnel.

But I don't think we should be doing that at all.

When our politicians and pundits talk about light at the end of the tunnel, they mean the darkness will come to an end one day. It won't. When Theo, Matt and I finally kayaked out of the tunnel, bursting into the day, we breathed an exhausted sigh of relief. But the darkness was still there, behind us. The darkness doesn't go away just because we're not in it any more.

What we celebrate during the Christmas season is not our reaching the end of the tunnel, darkness defeated, our emergence into the light; it's the opposite of that: light *coming into* the darkness.

It might appear tiny and insignificant while we're in the tunnel, but the light guides us, draws us, and – of course – ultimately, embraces us. The light coming into the world is *not* at the end of the tunnel, distant and tantalising; it's right here, in the tunnel with us all along, a pearl – tiny, but of great value (Matthew 13.46).

> 'I am the light of the world. Whoever follows me will never walk in darkness but will have the light of life.'
>
> John 8.12

And this light of life is not like dazzling angels in the sky, or a star in the east, or those incandescent magnesium decoy flares that hang sometimes over Salisbury Plain. This light is not a decoy; it's the truth, and it's not coming from a celestial beyond, but a poor stable in a dark alley, a guttering flame in a rough terracotta lamp filled with fish oil. It's shining in the face of a loving mother.

We don't emerge from darkness into light. We *are* the dark; the light emerges into us.

. . . . .

CHURCHES DEDICATED TO ST MICHAEL the archangel tend to be sited over pagan sacred places, on high ground. But this St Michael's – built in the twelfth century from flint and stone – sits almost hidden within a deep fold of the downs above a stream where a mill turned once and where, until a few years ago, there were watercress beds. In all likelihood, the present church replaced an older building on the same spot. It would be reasonable to assume Christmases have been celebrated here for a millennium and a half. And I'd hazard none of them have been quite like this.

For a start, at Holy Communion on Christmas morning we're not in St Michael's at all, but gathered outside in the churchyard around the lychgate. Sun not yet risen above the downs, the frost here is keen and deep; we stamp our feet, breath coming out of us like we're kettles boiling. It's on account of our breath that we're outside in the first place: our breath is a biohazard. There are too many of us to go inside the church where infection could be spread. So, out in the cold, standing well apart, we sing 'See amid the winter's snow' and 'In the bleak midwinter' and 'Hark, the herald'. Thus, we remain within the rules.

As I raise the round communion wafer at our makeshift altar and say 'We are one body because we all share in the one bread', the sun crests the line of hills behind the congregation and shines directly into my eyes. I could claim it was the brightness of the sun and the sharpness of the east wind that make my eyes water. But that wouldn't quite be true.

Later, my parents stand warming themselves around a fire in our garden. We struggle to hold champagne glasses while wearing gloves, and exchange presents like they're ticking bombs. We don't go inside together or eat a meal together or hug one another, or kiss.

The temptation to break the rules instead of our hearts

is enormous. Tipped off by a neighbour, a policeman knocked at a parishioner's door last week and inquired about her plans to have guests down from London over Christmas. The officer promised to return – as though out of consideration – to check she was complying with the rules: no guests staying. The illicit invitee was her son whom she hadn't seen all year. The rules.

What is it that makes us obey rules that run counter to our deepest wishes and desires? Perhaps it's just the threat: a policeman's knock, fear of prosecution or censure. A curtain twitching in a neighbour's window.

Or we might obey rules through obligation to some authority, the Bible perhaps, or legal precedent or a written constitution. Thomas Hobbes (1588–1679), a local hero (or monster, depending on your point of view), endeavoured to construct a political philosophy not on authority or precedent, but on rational, scientific foundations. Without enforceable rules or laws grounded in reason, Hobbes thinks, human life descends into a state of nature. And in a state of nature 'the life of man [is] solitary, poor, nasty, brutish, and short' – everyone for themselves and the devil take the hindmost. The terms of a peace treaty in this war are derived from what Hobbes calls the Laws of Nature. We permit the law to inhibit us because a free-for-all is no freedom at all.

According to Hobbes, the first law of nature is 'to seek peace and follow it'. In peace, human beings afford themselves security and safety. Deriving from this fundamental law, Hobbes argues, is the second law of nature:

That a man be willing... to lay down this right to all

things, and be contented with so much liberty against other men, as he would allow other men against himself.

At the heart of Hobbes's political thought is this axiomatic claim that the proper functioning of human intercourse in any field is essentially reciprocal. Hobbes offers a description of this reciprocity as a rational, mutually beneficial and enforceable contract. But you could just as easily express it as a command:

'In everything do to others as you would have them do to you; for this is the law and the prophets.'

Matthew 7.12

In our solipsistic, self-isolated and fragmented lives – particularly in our anonymised, online lives – it's all too easy to see ourselves in a Hobbesian war of everyone against everyone, as entirely at liberty, living out our 'right to all things', choosing to do as we please rather than to submit to shared laws which 'determine and bind' one and all.

But real freedom is neither war of all against all, nor is it underwritten by contractual obligation, but by love:

For you were called to freedom, brothers and sisters; only do not use your freedom as an opportunity for self-indulgence, but through love become slaves to one another.

Galatians 5.13

Outside St Michael's in the winter sun on Christmas morning, we pledge to live in love and peace with all, slaves to one another; and we acknowledge our oneness in the bread of life (John 6.35). Ultimately, freedom is not found in breaking loose, or breaking rules, but in breaking bread, in sharing. Paradoxically, true freedom, like love, is found in mutual surrender. Perhaps this is casuistry on my part, but I try to abide by the current rules, not according to some Hobbesian contract I enter into with my neighbour, but because I love my neighbour.

.....

IN THE LEE OF THE DOWNS the frost hasn't lifted for days, and here and there braids of frozen-melted-frozen snow still hem the north-facing fringes of the hedgerows. The sepulchral cawing of crows in the black branches of dead ash trees. Bitten fields, windswept downs, bare spinneys – all familiar enough, but these are borderlands suddenly.

Standing at the edge of an icy dew pond high on the hill, Nick and I look into a neighbouring valley. 'It's tier four down there,' he says. 'You can't go in. Or you can, but if you do, you can't come out again.' Mist slowly tamps the valley from the east.

Of course there are no roadblocks or rolls of barbed wire. But this is a border nonetheless. Our thoughts have been focussed on borders recently, what with queuing lorries at channel ports, motorways backing up. We talk of *our* borders, but really we are theirs. Where are you from? And I guarantee your answer presupposes a system of borders. Borders parcel up nations and persons neatly, yet they're ambiguous places – facing both ways, like Janus the Roman god of doorways, entrances and exits, comings and goings, and for whom January is named. This time of year is two-faced.

I remember how thrilling it was as a child, crossing borders with my parents. Guards with guns at their hips, Dad handing our passports through a car window to unsmiling customs officers. Cross a line on a map and the language changes, currency too. Food and architecture, even the faces of the people, are different on the other side.

Bo and Luke Duke racing their Chrysler Dodge across the Hazzard county line, to freedom. Borders are glamorous.

The truth is, I love borders; a luxury on my part, I know. I've never been stopped at one, or turned back. Others are all the time. Borders are barriers, pervious to the privileged. There's a moment in Evelyn Waugh's historical novel, *Helena*, when the future Emperor Constantius surveys the walled border at the edge of the Roman Empire. 'I love the wall', he says, Trump-style, to his young wife, who has left Britannia for the first time.

> Inside, peace, decency, the law, the altars of the Gods, industry, the arts, order; outside, wild beasts and savages, forest and swamp, bloody mumbo-jumbo, men like wolf packs.

You can keep the Roman side, frankly. It sounds dull as a dew pond. Constantius is a stone-cold prig. I find myself longing for 'outside', for beasts and savages. And some

Roman-hearted types would say mumbo-jumbo is my day job.

But for me or any of us to be 'outside' requires there to be an inside too, and a border between. The border is necessary for the romance. The Greeks understood this. They built temples in edge places, where land meets sea or sky or enemy. Named for the piles of stones that marked a boundary between territories, their god, Hermes, was born at the border. And yet he's a trickster, a traveller, a messenger, an inveterate crosser of borders. So, the very idea of a border is bound up with transgression. Where would smugglers be without border guards and customs inspectors? Bo and Luke without Boss Hogg and Sheriff Rosco?

Constantius' wall doesn't keep the beasts and savages out so much as it keeps them in our nightmares, secretly in our hearts, and keeps the smuggler and moonshiner in business. (Ultimately, it doesn't keep anyone out at all. Thank God.)

In Matthew's gospel, there's an early incursion across a border, from 'out there'. Wise Men come from the east. In the Greek, they come *apo anatolōn* – from where the sun rises, the orient. More than gold, frankincense and myrrh, they bring with them the mystery and allure of a crossed border, of 'outside'. The homespun shepherds are balanced by the exotic magi; their foreignness is essential to the story. Near and far meet in a stable. They do not cancel each other out, but affirm one another.

If the Christ child is to be 'born in us today', as the carol has it, then we need to accommodate in ourselves, as that stable does, both the familiar and the strange, the near and the far, the homely and the remote. In short, we need to live always at a border between this world and a kingdom that is coming, and already among us. It's a border running through all things. You don't need documents to cross over; creeds and catechisms won't help you. But you do need, like the magi, to have faith, and to have the courage and curiosity to make the crossing in the first place.

As we cross into a New Year, we proceed like the wise men, with the border always before us.

> 'I am the gate. Whoever enters by me will be saved, and will come in and go out and find pasture.'
>
> John 10.9

There's no gate in Constantius' wall, but there is in your heart. Wherever, and whenever, you stand you're always at the border, at the gate.

> Lord,
> you called Jeremiah to the gates (Jeremiah 17.19):
> draw us, like him, to the margins,
> to new places where our certainties crumble away,
>     our hearts are opened
>     and we are to live by faith alone.
> Grant us your grace that we might
>     abide always in your promise,
>     walk always in your peace,
>     and enter through the living Gate,
> even Jesus Christ your Son our Lord. AMEN

. . . . .

SISTER MARY IS MOVING, and days after Christmas too, just the worst time of the year. She and her fellow sisters in the Community of St John Baptist, sometimes called the Clewer Sisters, have been living happily for years at Ripon College Cuddesdon, outside Oxford. To see Mary and Ann, last surviving sisters in the community, leaving the college is sad. Their daily round of prayer and devotion, their presence in college, is like an operating system. The college will need to find an entirely new way of functioning without them. A reboot will be required.

When I was a student at the college myself, Mary and I would often sneak out of the common room and smoke our way through a packet of fags, drinking red wine and putting the world to rights.

Before becoming a nun, Mary worked as a teacher in the East End of London. She was married to a jazz journalist and tells everyone she meets how she once shook Count Basie's hand. 'Marriage,' she says, 'was wonderful to get into, and equally wonderful to get out of.' Through the 1980s, she nursed a dear friend as he died of AIDS. After that, Mary followed a call from God to life in community. And she's gently, gracefully been doing God's work ever since. It's a long way from the White Hart, her uncle's pub where she grew up, on the Thames estuary at Greenhithe in Kent.

When Emma was ill with Covid back in March, Sister Mary sent her a shawl she'd knitted. And she's been a third grandmother to all my children. For years, Aggie would exchange letters and postcards with Mary about books she was reading. Sister Mary has a deep appreciation of children's literature. She introduced Aggie and me to Alan

Garner, for which I will always be grateful. We in turn tried to win her round to the *Anne of Green Gables* books, but failed. She found Anne irritating.

Mary has an encyclopaedic memory for salacious, faux-Chaucerian folk songs into which, after a glass or two of port, she is liable to launch. Chastity belts and stiff lances, lowering drawbridges and magnificent chargers. I've seen her reduce more than one bishop to tears with this filth, while a 'butter wouldn't melt' look remains on her face throughout. Howls of laughter and Mary is all: what? Oh, please –.

Joey took to Sister Mary immediately. I put that down, partly, to an encounter he had with a nun at a very impressionable age. He was about six months old, and Emma and I had taken him with us to visit friends in Salamanca for Easter. One afternoon, we were trundling Joey in his pushchair around the extraordinary plateresque cloisters of the Convento de las Dueñas when a nun leapt out from behind the counter where she was selling the convent's speciality almond biscuits. A towering vision in black and white with thick spectacles and wrestler's hands, she loomed over him: '¡O qué rico es!' she exclaimed and pushed her huge face close to his. I thought he'd bawl in terror; even I was pretty alarmed. But Joey just beamed. The nun was entranced. She said a prayer in Spanish and gave us a box of biscuits. I'll never forget her.

Nor will Joey. Perhaps, many years later, he sees that first nun in Mary. He wants to come with me to visit Mary in her new home as soon as the restrictions are lifted. I don't think I've yet felt so cut off as I do now, unable to go to a pub with Sister Mary for a Christmas drink and a gossip.

Long ago, playing Oswald in a touring production of Ibsen's *Ghosts*, I found myself regularly trapped in digs around the country with the actor playing Engstrand. He was a disreputable old ham who used to tell anybody who'd listen how he'd once had sex with a nun against the tomb of Admiral Nelson in the crypt at St Paul's. I didn't believe him. (As far as I recall, the audience didn't believe him as Engstrand either.)

Underlying the actor's boast is a popular trope, that nuns appear inviolable yet are voracious. In sixteenth- and seventeenth-century Venice, a surfeit of aristocratic young women filled the city's convents. Families who couldn't afford to keep up in the marriage market were forced to consign un-dowry-able daughters to the veil. The erotic potential in such a situation was not wasted on the world. Nuns are a recurring male fantasy. If you want proof, google 'naughty nun' and browse the costumes, or go back to Boccaccio (1313–1375):

> There are a great many men and women who are so dense as to be firmly convinced that when a girl takes the white veil and dons the black cowl, she ceases to be a woman or to experience feminine longings, as though the very act of making her a nun had caused her to turn into stone.

Even if the actor's story about the nun were true, it seems to me there's an awful irony in play here. The Clewer Sisters were established in 1852 to support and protect vulnerable and exploited women, sex workers in particular. Nuns, these objects of male fantasy, are actually busy working in an environment where those fantasies have done most damage.

Far from being hidden or hived off from the world, the Clewer Sisters were out working in the community. There's nothing secretive or secluded about Sister Mary or the nun at Las Dueñas. Quite the reverse, they are 'of the world' in a far richer and more open way than so-called worldly folk like 'Engstrand'. Sister Mary's loving, wise engagement with everyone she meets is a far cry from that uniquely male blend of the cocksure and the clandestine.

It seems to me, instead, that the real way to be, the real way to live, is nun-like: to look out at the world and everyone in it with a glorious, thankful *¡Qué rico es!'*

.....

AS A CHILD, when I went to stay at my grandmother's house, I was always drawn to a particular picture that hung in the room where I slept at the end of a nursery corridor. It was a gloomy black-and-white etching of a desert landscape at night. Dominating the rocky foreground were two prowling lions. Beyond them, quite far off, on the horizon, human figures: a man leading a donkey on which a woman sat, head bowed, the little group surrounded by a halo of light. Perhaps they're silhouetted by the moon, I thought; perhaps not. Perhaps the glow belongs to them.

The sinuous muscularity of the lions, the long shadows and treeless landscape: the picture had a portentous quality, and I was frightened of it. But I knew it depicted the Flight into Egypt, that the woman and man were Mary and Joseph, and that the infant Jesus was somewhere hidden in the folds of Mary's cloak.

Was I told it was a picture of the Flight into Egypt or is there something so deeply coded into our shared cultural inheritance that these visual ingredients: a man on foot, a nursing mother on a donkey are just unmistakably telling *that* story? Narrative grows around the edges of this image like fruit around a seed. And we know too, somehow, that these elements – man, woman, child, donkey – are characters in a story full of fear. The figures in the picture are running away from something terrible.

I suppose it was around this time last year – early January or thereabouts – that I first remember hearing and learning new terms: 'coronavirus' and 'Covid-19'. In the intervening twelve months, we've all lived through our own flights from danger, doing our best – like Joseph – to protect those we love. And here we are again, apparently in more danger than ever, still on the run. Imagine looking up at one of those old split-flap destination display boards in an airport, all the letters cascading through their alphabetical permutations, and all settling on 'Egypt'. Suddenly, all flights are flights into Egypt. We're all running from something terrible, seeking safety. Lockdown isn't fixed; it's flight.

> O God, make speed to save us.
> O Lord, make haste to help us.

The picture now hangs in my house. I'm not frightened of it any more. And I discovered yesterday, as I took it off the wall in preparation for a bit of lockdown painting and decorating, that there's a brass plaque on the back of the frame. The picture was a gift to my grandfather when he was a boy. Perhaps it was a confirmation present. The plaque has a quote:

> The beloved of the Lord shall dwell in safety
> and the Lord shall cover them all the day long.
>
> Deuteronomy 33.12

And suddenly the meaning of the picture is reversed: the lions in the foreground are not hunting, poised to pounce; they're slinking away. They recognise something in the light covering the new family. That light in the darkness is shining on them too. The male lion turns to look back, I now see, almost protectively.

Herbert Thomas Dicksee, the Victorian artist who created the picture, was famous in his day for drawings of dogs and horses. I imagine the motivation behind his painting the scene was the opportunity it afforded of rendering the lions; and they're brilliantly done. We can somehow sense their confusion, skirting this fleeing family, not daring to approach or attack for reasons they themselves find baffling, unfathomable.

Of course, the real subject of the picture is not the lions, but the infant, hidden, in the distance, under his mother's cloak. And in the biblical story too, with its mass-murdering tyrant, angels appearing in dreams, foreign lands, foreign kings, stars and portents, it's easy to miss the child at the centre of it all.

Look out at the world: lions everywhere. Lions prowling empty streets and shopping centres and departure lounges. Lions skulking in the shadows around vacant service station car parks, beyond the floodlights and drive-thrus. Lions roaming our villages.

Nonetheless, at the heart of the story of the Flight into Egypt is a vision of safety. Because safety doesn't mean absence of risk. And you can be safe without knowing it. Joseph and Mary fleeing through the desert at night, pursued by a tyrant, feel desperately unsafe. But they are safe, thanks to that which seems most vulnerable and weak.

As we enter another lockdown, perhaps we need to turn the picture over, to see what's written on the back of everything. To find the reality: that we are loved, that we dwell in safety wherever we are, and however unsafe everything feels. What looks like a desert is the way to freedom. And what looks like darkness is the dawn.

.....

WHEN I WENT TO START THE CAR this morning to drive to a funeral in Salisbury, the battery was flat, and the interior shrouded in a thick layer of mould. The upholstery (if it can be called that) is spotted and blotched green, blue and grey, the steering wheel haloed in a fine, white fungus. And here and there the dashboard bristles with something filamenty, like frost. Actually, it's quite beautiful.

But I decide to use Emma's car.

The journey takes me across the downs from the Kennet Valley, up and over, and into the Collingbournes. There are two villages called Collingbourne. One is Ducis, the other Kingston. It's said that in the seventeenth century, the Collingbournes were on opposite sides in the Civil War. Ducis was parliamentarian, while the more northerly

Kingston, true to its name, sided with the king. Nearly four hundred years later, there remains a buried undercurrent of antagonism. You wouldn't notice it immediately, but scratch the surface and old rivalries linger, albeit harmlessly now. Actually, I think any vestige of hostility is more likely to stem from cricket, or the fiercely contested inter-village tournament. Last year – and I'm deadly serious here – trouble broke out with accusations of cheating in the speed knitting competition.

In spite of these ructions, what keeps the communities rubbing along more or less peaceably is a slowly re-established neighbourliness, a patina built up over generations of cooperation and quid pro quo, of facing adversities together, sharing bus routes and secondary schools, and vicars. Like mould growing, softening everything, the slow accrual of years blurs and eventually effaces any sharp contours of political difference.

We're too quick, I think, to see this sort of process as a masking, a concealing, an obscuring; to think original truth is always underneath, hidden and hard, like my car's upholstery. But truth can be on the surface too, growing over things like mould. There's nothing especially truthful about origins.

Perhaps Civil War is on my mind because of the scenes in Washington this week, when Donald Trump's supporters 'stormed' the Capitol. (Reporters keep saying they 'stormed' the Capitol. Watching the footage back, it's frankly more of a drizzling than a storming.) But listen to these protestors or insurrectionists being interviewed and you hear the same thing over and over again – they know the truth has been covered up, buried, denied, stolen.

In his encounter with the Church at Corinth, St Paul comes face to face with precisely these sorts of problems. He admonishes members of the church who lay claim to special knowledge.

> If you think that you are wise in this age, you should become fools so that you may become wise. For the wisdom of this world is foolishness with God.
>
> 1 Corinthians 3.18–19

What the Corinthians have adopted, and what Trump's supporters often express when interviewed, is a form of Gnosticism. Gnosticism is a family of ideas, but near its root is the notion that the truth is known only to a few. The rest of us are ignorant, uninitiated dupes. The Truth (capital T) has been hidden from most of humanity, but those who are enlightened, who can see past fake news or the vested interests of orthodoxy, have gained access to a saving Secret (capital S). Gnosticism is conspiracy theorising elevated to the status of philosophy or theology, and it develops in the form of cults and sects: it divides. The church at Corinth is a divided church, a church in a state of civil war.

We all have a gnostic tendency, easily gulled into thinking the Truth is difficult to find, hidden from us in history, or by 'elites'. We even assume the Truth might be inaccessible to us because of our human faculties. Metaphysicians and scientists sometimes tell us ultimate reality (whatever that is) can be adequately described only when we remove ourselves from the description. But this is obviously false. My experience of the world is part of the world along with everything else. To get at the Truth, we're told, requires us (absurdly) to transcend our humanity, to learn arcane lore, a special language. This Truth does not set you free (John 8.32), it sets you apart.

Dealing with the fractious Corinthians, Paul takes a different approach. He tells them he did not come 'proclaiming the mystery of God to you in lofty words or wisdom'. Instead, he came 'in weakness and in fear and in much trembling' (1 Corinthians 2.1-5).

Paul offers an approach to the world that does not pretend to privileged access to knowledge. It's this approach that is described by one of the early Church Fathers, Irenaeus, writing in the second century. It is better, he says,

> that one should have no knowledge whatever of any one reason why a single thing in creation has been made, but should believe in God and continue in his love, than that, puffed up through knowledge of this kind, he should fall away from that love which is the life of man.

Claims to special knowledge all too easily wrench us away from the shared love which is our life. Worldly, gnostic Truth is liable to divide us into Ducis and Kingston, left and right, saved and damned. Whether we're in Collingbourne or standing on the Capitol:

> We must no longer be children, tossed to and fro and blown about by every wind of doctrine, by people's trickery, by their craftiness in deceitful scheming. But speaking the truth in love, we must grow up in every

way into him who is the head, into Christ.

Ephesians 4.14–15

Let the truth grow on us, grow over us and through us – and we'll find it's ultimately expressible and understandable only in love.

. . . . .

BACK IN MARCH LAST YEAR, John sent me a piece of writing in which he talked about 'the fibres of his being becoming attuned to the dance of glory'. John died just before Christmas. I'll miss him very much, not least because we never managed to have our long-planned conversation about the Greek philosopher, Plotinus (205–270).

On the morning I hear of John's death, it's announced that Debenhams is going out of business. John would've enjoyed the coincidence: Debenhams offers the only instance, as far as I know, of ancient philosophy meeting modern retail. Bear with me...

Towards the end of 1908, a translation into English of a tractate by Plotinus called *On Beauty*, was published by a small independent press. The translation was made, not by a Greek scholar from a book-lined study in All Souls', but by a restless thirty-six-year-old Irish journalist called Stephen MacKenna. Troubled by poor health, an unhappy marriage and the pressures of making a living by his pen, MacKenna lacked the leisure for scholarship. He didn't even have a university degree.

In 1905, while covering the First Russian Revolution for the *New York World*, MacKenna had happened upon a

Greek edition of Plotinus in a backstreet bookseller's in St Petersburg. He was immediately transfixed. From that moment, he set his mind to translating all the philosopher's work. Holed up in his St Petersburg digs, he writes about his first encounter with Plotinus in his journal. 'It seems to me,' he says, 'that I must be born for him.'

Following its publication, MacKenna's *On Beauty* vanished without trace. Until, four years later, he received a letter from Sir Ernest Debenham, who was then running his family's retail empire, asking him when he might expect a complete translation of Plotinus. For the remainder of MacKenna's life, Debenham was a benefactor, patron and friend.

In a letter to Debenham, Dr T.E. Page, an eminent classicist of the early twentieth century, said, 'You could possibly find half a dozen scholars who could translate Plotinus accurately; but to reproduce him, to make him live again, to catch something of that unearthly beauty that attaches to his words – this needs something more than accuracy or scholarship, and Mr MacKenna possesses it.' The editor of the *London Mercury*, Sir John Squire wrote, 'I do not think that any living man has written nobler prose than Mr MacKenna.'

In a memoir of MacKenna, E.R. Dodds wrote of his friend's work and of Debenham's support:

> It is a noble monument to an Irishman's courage, an Englishman's generosity, and the idealism of both; and it is one of the very few great translations of our day.

Thanks to Debenham's support, work on Plotty (as

MacKenna affectionately referred to Plotinus) was finally completed in 1930. MacKenna had four years left to live. 'My work isn't much,' he wrote, 'but it stands done: now on milk and eggs and with music and Irish I can idle and wait in peace of conscience.'

MacKenna's translation of Plotinus' *Enneads* is still in print, and it is a masterpiece. John loved it – and so do I. This is a quote from the final tractate:

> God is outside of none, present unperceived to all; we break away from Him, or rather from ourselves; a child distraught will not recognize its father; to find ourselves is to know our source.

Perhaps what moves me most about MacKenna's story is the example it offers of what James Joyce (also an admirer of Mackenna's writing) calls an 'epiphany', a sudden – and sometimes spiritual – recognition that what lies before us, however apparently inconsequential, is burdened with profound, life-changing significance: a chance find in a second-hand bookshop, a pair of butterflies at the church window, a thumb-print in clay, raindrops on barbed wire. While at first they may appear quite trivial, these conjunctions of events are 'thin places', moments when a kingdom can be glimpsed through the gauze of everyday experience. It seems to me, our lives are punctuated and patterned by these pinch points, these epiphanies, and we need to be awake to their graceful force, and willing to follow where they lead, back to our source, our Father.

Epiphany, of course, has a technical meaning: the manifestation of Jesus' divinity as Christ, the Word of God. But actually biblical Epiphany and Joyce's literary equivalent are closely related. Throughout the season of Epiphany, Jesus is revealed as the Son of God in *detail*, as a baby in a filthy stable, an infant brought to the temple by poor parents. His divinity is found in the form of a dove, in the taste of wine at a wedding, a face in the crowd, a passer-by.

I remember once taking a sixth-form student to meet John. Enrolled in an educational charity programme, this student was depressed; he felt disregarded and obsolete in an (expensive) educational system that rewarded all talents and gifts but his own, advancing everyone but him. He wanted to be a writer, a poet. John was kind to him, listened to him, took him seriously in a way no one else had hitherto.

They sat under an apple tree in John's garden and spoke for over an hour. Afterwards, the young man was transformed, dazzled by John's wisdom and encouragement. In a real sense, he'd found himself, known his source. That student is now at university studying creative writing, and he's thriving.

You can pick up a book in a market, listen to this wise man talking under an apple tree, taste a certain wine at a wedding, or meet this bloke by the sea while mending your nets. And you can find – quite suddenly – your being is attuned to the dance of glory.

.....

BARRELLING THROUGH LAST NIGHT from the West, a storm left us without power all evening and into the small hours. We cooked, ate and crept to bed by candlelight, Victorian for a few hours. But in the middle of the night, we were pitched peremptorily back into the twenty-first century by radio, TV, WiFi, and lights blazing.

Next morning, the late-January sun has a rinsing, searchlight quality; it's revelatory. I see suddenly how dusty the house is, how grubby the windows and dirty the floors. It's like waking up to reality, waking from a dream.

And I've been dreaming a lot recently. Every night is busy. Bright yellow parakeets, and a huge topiary key, trying to write an urgent message using bits of broken china, argy-bargy in a cinema queue, and I'm searching for my shoes so I can follow Aggie out onto this narrow, sagging bridge across a river. I turn to face what's been pursuing me. It's only a child, I think, as it steps out of the darkness of my parents' bedroom doorway.

Not nightmares exactly, although some are uncanny. Apparently I'm not alone. Many people have been experiencing something similar during lockdown, an unexpected and widespread rash of vivid dreaming. Imagine being able somehow to visualise this: a locked-down planet Earth enveloped in a swirling spore cloud of dreams. Trapped in our homes, our minds wander free, refusing quarantine. And we're fleeing every night on strange, solitary diasporas, like lost souls in those medieval doom paintings.

The prophet Joel describes God speaking to the people who have returned to him:

'I will pour out my spirit on all flesh;
your sons and your daughters shall prophesy,
your old men shall dream dreams
and your young men shall see visions.'

Joel 2.28

Where do these dreams we dream come from? And what do they mean? When Scrooge puts his dreamlike visitation from Marley down to a 'bit of undigested beef', he's actually half-quoting Aristotle, who suggested dreams might be the result of indigestion. Thomas Hobbes similarly ascribes dreaming to 'the agitation of the inward parts of man's body'.

In the twentieth century, we were taught that our dreams come, not from our bodies so much as our restless, traumatised minds. So, Freud sets us nightly adrift on the troubled waters of the unconscious; Jung claims our dreams are populated with archetypes and primordial motifs that express our collective unconscious.

I suppose the thinking goes like this: if we know where our dreams come from, what causes them, then we can give a plausible if reductive description of what they are: indigestion, agitation, childhood trauma or repressed desires (Freud), the buried psychic life of our ancestors (Jung). What we're being offered here, what the books from a 'Mind, Body, Spirit' section of any bookshop can offer, are explanations of what dreams are, and interpretations of what they mean.

But Joel in those verses doesn't offer any explanation. Dreams aren't explained, or interpreted or understood: dreams are dreamed. They are the gift of the Holy Spirit, nudging us into a space where our explanations, interpretations and analyses all fall short, where we are pitched into the middle of things. That should disquiet us. That's the prophet's point.

In the introduction to his 1827 lectures on the philosophy of religion, Hegel (1770–1831) describes religion as:

The absolute object. It is the region of eternal truth and eternal virtue, where all the riddles of thought, all contradictions, and all the sorrows of the heart should show themselves to be resolved.

Would someone please tell the Holy Spirit? Because at Pentecost, when the Holy Spirit descends on the apostles in tongues of flame, and when Peter quotes those verses from Joel (Acts 2.17), religion does not appear to be an 'absolute object', an answer to every question. Rather, it is wildly unsettling and transformative, more of a riddle than a resolution.

Believed by some and dismissed by many, the Holy Spirit certainly doesn't come giving a plausible account of itself or clarification or guidance as to how it is to be interpreted.

When Hegel talks of religion as absolute object, he's doing what Scrooge does when he ascribes Marley to a morsel of beef. He's offering to pin the ghost down, to reduce it to something more or less graspable, more or less digestible. Hegel's philosophy of religion is crystalline rather than combustible. But the lived reality of religious faith is often turbulent, troubling and unpredictable. Like dreams.

Dreams, like prophecies, like faith itself, put us on notice: we're not standing on high, masterly subjects of our experiences, above the world as object spread out helpfully below. We're in the swim, permeable parts of an unfolding creation. Lived experience is stormy, spirited and swirling. We are spirit-tossed.

The Holy Spirit just comes. Like dreams, like breath,

like life. So, dream, breathe, live. You don't need instructions. Which is just as well, because there aren't any.

.....

IN THE VALLEY BELOW St James' church there's a path that runs between steep downs and into the woods. After a mile or so, you leave the woods by a pond, and climb through grazing sheep and past game coverts to a copse where the footpath meets one of the many ancient tracks that criss-cross this area.

With hindsight, it might not have been the best afternoon for walking. The weather came in around three o' clock, snowflakes drifting through the trees above our heads and twisting up to meet us out of tea-brown puddles at our feet. On open, unwooded stretches, the hills all around are lost behind a busy scrim of falling snow.

Hoods pulled low and walking boots beginning to let in water, we eventually arrived at a crossroads where the track meets the Ridgeway, a route that runs along the top of the downs here. To medieval sheep drovers, this would've been a busy intersection. Today, the crossroads is deserted and silent, snow accumulating in ruts and hollows and between the roots of trees.

Half a mile away to the east is Gallows Hill, named for its gibbet on which, in 1676, the lovers George Broomham and Dorothy Newman were hanged for the murder of George's wife, Martha, and their son, Robert. Crossroads always seem to amass for themselves gruesome legends: murders, executions and meetings with the devil.

Alright, that's an exaggeration; most crossroads are

unstained and innocent. Think of American cities where crossroads are effectively addresses. I've just got off the bus and I'm standing on the corner of Eighth and Fortieth. A New Yorker knows exactly where I am. Crossroads are orientations, grid references.

But out here, things are a little different; crossroads confront you. Crossroads put you on your mettle; a decision will have to be made. Getting lost might start here. Crossroads present us with problems. Even Hercules is unmanned at a crossroads, dithering.

The Stoic philosopher, Chrysippus (279–206 BC), thinks animals understand this. He describes a dog on the scent of a rabbit. Nose to the ground, Rex races after his prey along a track – until he reaches a crossroads. Drat. Now there are three possible routes the rabbit could have taken, Chrysippus tells us. Sniffing, Rex hurries down the left-hand path but quickly loses the scent and doubles back. At the crossroads again, Rex sniffs and now chooses the middle path, but loses the scent a second time. Returning to the crossroads, Rex doesn't even bother to sniff out the trail, hurling himself down the right-hand path. And catches the rabbit.

Chrysippus' point is that Rex is capable of what the Stoics called syllogistic reasoning. Rex's thinking at the crossroads takes the form of a disjunctive syllogism, and goes like this: either x or y or z. But not x, and not y. Therefore z. Rex doesn't need to confirm his decision by sniffing: it *must* be the right-hand path.

Our problem is, we sometimes reach a crossroads without a rabbit running helpfully before us. There's no scent or signpost, no helpful bystander with a 'he went thaddaway'. We think of Robert Frost and his sigh. Faced by two paths in the forest, he took:

> The one less travelled by
> and that has made all the difference.

Crossroads make a difference.

We're standing at a crossroads now, faced by difference. We've left Christmas and Epiphany behind; in front of us is Lent. And here we are, at this fork in the year. More than ever, the Church calendar seems to be perfectly in step with the national (and international) situation. Daily, we're watching lines on a graph – rates of vaccination and rates of infection – that will cross, their trajectories heading, we hope, in opposite directions. We're approaching a crossroads, a turning point.

In Matthew's gospel, Jesus tells a story about a king who invites friends to a wedding banquet for his son. But the ungrateful guests snub the king and fail to show up. So the king sends messengers out into the community to invite people willy-nilly to the feast, 'everyone you find', he says (Matthew 22.9). The king tells his messengers:

> 'Go ye therefore unto the partings of the highways, and as many as ye shall find, bid to the marriage feast.'
>
> Matthew 22.9

In other words, the king calls us to his banquet from the crossroads, from the place where the ways of the world confront us, from decisive and divergent places that make all the difference. In short: from where we are. At the partings, at the crossroads, is where we're lost and found.

When two of Jesus' disciples are hurrying away from Jerusalem after the crucifixion, a stranger comes and walks with them. This stranger turns out to be a living crossroads, a perpetual prompt to turn back, to make a choice. The disciples must learn – we all must learn – that even the widest, easiest road (Matthew 7.13–14) is actually an infinite series of crossroads. You can always turn in at the Gate.

To be on the Way (the oldest name for the Christian faith) is to be facing a cross. It makes all the difference.

.....

END OF THE ROAD for the Ibiza. It failed its MOT last week, and now I'm faced with a dilemma: stump up for repairs, or have a word with Barry in the next village. He'd give me fifty quid for the car (a good price, honestly), and it'd be consigned to the towering stack of scrap at the metal merchants' on the road to Pewsey.

Why am I torn? It's just a car after all. Marie Kondo is an 'organisational consultant', the queen of decluttering, a publishing sensation, with her own hugely successful syndicated TV shows. Perhaps I should apply her famous test and ask myself: does the Ibiza spark joy? If it does, pay for the repairs. If it doesn't...

Truthfully, it doesn't. It barely sparks at all. As a car, the Ibiza is absolute Balearics.

But I don't subscribe for a moment to the Marie Kondo method. Whether or not the car sparks joy in me is surely beside the point. I've been through stuff with this car, and I don't mean puddles, thunderstorms and snow drifts. I mean personal stuff. There are still scrunched-up fag packets in the side pocket; I gave up years and years ago. Aggie (or 'Agi') has crayoned her name on the passenger door panel; she's taking her GCSEs this summer, or should be (and can now spell her name correctly). There's a road map of France on the back seat, from the days before Google or Waze. An old football boot from when Theo played leftback for the Ramsbury Under 12s; he's at university. *Slow Train Coming* on CD, scratched and unplayable, still in the slot. This car is history. It's archaeological.

The only decent car I ever owned was a blue-grey 1975 Mercedes saloon. I bought it off a family two streets down from where I was living at the time. As I drove the car away, I remember catching sight of the little daughter crying on the pavement outside her house. I don't think she was crying because the car had brought her joy. She was crying because she felt connected to the car. It had taken her on holiday; she'd smiled at her mother in its rearview on the drive to her first day at school; she'd lost chewy sweets between its sweaty leatherette seats. She had a relationship with the car, as I do with the Ibiza. It needn't be joyful, but it is meaningful.

(The Merc proved to be a rust bucket, its chassis a sieve. Driving down the M4 in the rain on a first date with Emma, the car filled with muddy water up to our ankles. Reader, she married me. I can't imagine why.)

But I think my point stands. It's not that things do or don't bring us joy; it's that, like the little girl who cried, we invest our feelings and ourselves in stuff. We commit to the contents of the world, and we feel the world committing back. You might say, Colin, it's just a car, an inanimate object. But then I'd ask, how do you feel about your wedding ring, or those christening cufflinks, that silver-backed hairbrush? We are meaning-making creatures, and we make meaning everywhere, and out of everything. Don't we?

Well, no. I don't think we do. Ask yourself this: do we actually make meaning, or do we find it? Is it the investment of our feelings that makes the world meaningful for us, or do we invest our feelings because the world is meaningful in itself? For Christians, for people of all faiths, this admits of an easy answer.

> Let the heavens be glad, and let the earth rejoice;
>     let the sea roar, and all that fills it;
>     let the field exult, and everything in it.
> Then shall all the trees of the forest sing for joy.
>                                   Psalm 96.11–12

It's not that I take joy in the trees of the forest (although I do); it's that they are themselves joy-full. Hard-nosed, we could say the psalmist is speaking poetically or adopting a *Toy Story*-style anthropomorphism. But I think the psalm and the *Toy Story* films are both expressing a deep truth: that meaning is not mine to make; joy is not mine to take. They are both there in everything, for me to find and share. The sky is glad, the forest sings.

We knew this as children; now we need to relearn it, and not, I suggest, from an 'organisational consultant'.

> Ask the animals, and they will teach you;
>     the birds of the air, and they will tell you;
>     ask the plants of the earth, and they will teach you;

and the fish of the sea will declare to you.
Who among all these does not know
    that the hand of the Lord has done this?
In his hand is the life of every living thing
    and the breath of every human being.

Job 12.7–10

Creation is a work of joyful love: 'the earth is full of the steadfast love of the Lord' (Psalm 33.5). The essence of all things is the love of God.

All things. So, ask yourself: what *doesn't* spark joy?

. . . . .

IT'S ALMOST A YEAR since I was standing outside All Saints', watching the churchwarden lock the door.

Lockdown was a novel experience back then, and none of us could have known that a year later, we'd still be isolated from one another and trapped in our homes.

Here I am, still looking at a locked door, albeit one that opened now and then through the summer and autumn.

A second Lent in lockdown and we're beginning to look back and take stock. A recent article in the *Spectator* ('Holy Relic: What will be left of the Church of England after the Pandemic?' 6th February 2021) describes what followed the closing of our churches in Lent 2020: 'When Covid struck, and people turned to their churches for spiritual consolation, what did they find? Closed doors.'

I'm tempted to argue that this is simply false. I could point out how our churches have been helping to run food banks and organise local support networks, how they've been cooking and serving hot meals, answering helplines, working out how to deliver worship online, collecting prescriptions for housebound parishioners, burying our loved ones, and even sending out the occasional reflection. Above all, they've been praying. This doesn't sound like closed doors.

But actually, if I'm honest, as I sit on the wall, wrapped up against the cold, I rather like the idea of us all turning to our churches and finding closed doors. We wouldn't be the first to find the doors closed.

> When it was evening on that day, the first day of the week, and the doors of the house where the disciples had met were locked for fear of the Jews, Jesus came and stood among them and said, 'Peace be with you.'
>
> John 20.19

The Church begins with closed doors; it begins *behind* closed doors in the form of vulnerable and isolated individual people 'hoping against hope' (Romans 4.18).

In the gospel, the doors of the upper room are closed for fear of arrest and persecution. And Jesus doesn't demand the doors be unlocked and opened to him. That the doors are closed is a sensible precaution. It is also immaterial. He's already standing among them.

But if we read this passage as Jesus' *X-Files* capacity to walk through solid doors or walls, we haven't done it justice. Because in fact, he's not standing among the disciples at all; the disciples are *standing among him*. Jesus is not outside the doors; he's not outside anything. Rather, he is the outside *of* everything, the definition of all things.

We've all been standing in the midst of him from the beginning. The whole world in his hands.

So to talk about a church having closed doors is to talk from a world of locks and locksmiths, of real estate and risk assessments; it is to see the Church as an institution, not as the Body of Christ. This year we've been frightened, isolated, in danger and in grief: we've locked our doors. Now *that's* the Church. And where he was then, he is now.

In this part of the country, many of our village churches are built from flint ploughed out of the hills and carted down lanes and tracks to be mortared into walls, buttresses and stout towers. I love them, these repositories of prayer, these stone boxes in the bends and doubles of the down-land, like tufting buttons pinning us to this ancient landscape. With their Saxon fonts, recumbent crusaders, Victorian stained glass, they are dropped anchors, holding us on history's tide. When a storm blows in, as it has this year, we need that anchor. So I understand the concern and complaint expressed in the *Spectator* article.

But ultimately, it seems to me, it's not the Church's job to let people in, like a club; it's the Church's job to let us and the message out – into freedom, into one another, into a coming kingdom. The Church is a story, written with an end in mind; it is cupped and closed palms, a gilded cage, prison walls, even a mousetrap. When Joy unlocks the doors of All Saints', when the doors open again, they open not for us to enter, but for us to *escape*, like butterflies, into an infinitely deeper embrace.

# MUSIC

**MARLBOROUGH HIGH STREET – PAGE 213**
'Illuminated', Arto Lindsay, *Invoke* (Righteous Babe, 2002)

**A PASSAGE STRUCK ME – PAGE 216**
'Paul and Silas in Jail', Washington Philips, *The Key to the Kingdom* (Yazoo, 2005)

**IN THE DENTIST'S WAITING ROOM – PAGE 217**
'Waiting', John Cale, *Le Vent De La Nuit* (Crépuscule, 1999)

**FREEZING FOG – PAGE 220**
'Long Way Around the Sea', Low, *Christmas* (Kranky, 1999)

**EVERY YEAR WE FETCH DOWN – PAGE 223**
Will Oldham, 'Pushkin' on Palace Brothers, *Days in the Wake* (Drag City, 1994)

**BETWEEN THE HAMLET – PAGE 227**
'Rambunctious Cloud', Vic Chestnutt, *Ghetto Bells* (New West Records, 2005)

**FOR THE FIRST TIME IN A FEW DAYS – PAGE 230**
'Hosianna-Mantra', Popol Vuh, *Hosianna Mantra* (Pilz, 1972)

**WOULD YOU ALL PLEASE STAND – PAGE 234**
'Livin' on a Prayer', Bon Jovi, *Slippery When Wet* (Vertigo, 1986)

**ABOUT A HUNDRED METRES – PAGE 237**
'River of Heaven', Six Organs of Admittance, *Luminous Night* (Drag City, 2009)

**CHURCHES DEDICATED TO ST MICHAEL – PAGE 240**
Shirley Collins, vocalist, 'The Cherry Tree Carol', traditional, Shirley Collins, *Sweet England* (Argo, 1959)

IN THE LEE OF THE DOWNS – PAGE 244
'Border Lord', Kris Kirstofferson, *Border Lord* (Monument, 1972)

SISTER MARY IS MOVING – PAGE 248
'A Divine Image', David Axelrod, *Songs of Experience* (Capitol, 1969)

AS A CHILD – PAGE 251
'An teicheadh go hÉigipt', traditional, Anonymous 4, *Wolcum Yule: Celtic British Carols and Songs* (Harmonia Mundi, 2003)

WHEN I WENT TO START THE CAR – PAGE 254
'In Search of Truth', Lonnie Liston Smith and the Cosmic Echoes, *Astral Travelling* (Flying Dutchman, 1973)

BACK IN MARCH LAST YEAR – PAGE 258
'Unitive Knowledge of the Godhead', OM, *Pilgrimage* (Southern Lord, 2007)

BARRELLING THROUGH LAST NIGHT – PAGE 261
'Virtually So #2', Roy Montgomery and Chris Heaphy, *True* (Kranky, 1999)

IN THE VALLEY BELOW – PAGE 265
'Cross Road Blues – Take 2', Robert Johnson, *The Complete Recordings* (Columbia, 1990)

END OF THE ROAD – PAGE 268
'The Luckiest Guy on the Lower East Side', The Magnetic Fields, *69 Love Songs* (Merge, 1999)

IT'S ALMOST A YEAR – PAGE 271
Richard Strauss, Vier letzte Lieder, TrV:296:4: *Im Abendrot*, with Jessye Norman and the Gewandhausorchester, Leipzig, conducted by Kurt Masur, *Richard Strauss, Vier Letzte Lieder* (Philips, 2007)

*Acta Sanctorum*, ed. J. Bollandus & G. Henschenius, vol.34

Agamben, Giorgio, *Language and Death: The Place of Negativity*, translated by Karen E. Pinkus and Michael Hardt. (Minneapolis: University of Minnesota Press, 1991)

Anselm of Canterbury, *The Major Works*, (Oxford: Oxford University Press, 1998)

Anonymous, *The Cloud of Unknowing And Other Works*, translated by A.C. Spearing (London: Penguin, 2001)

Aristotle, *De Anima (On the Soul)*, translated by Hugh Lawson-Tancred (Oxford: Oxford University Press, 1996)
—— *Physics*, translated by Robin Waterfield (Oxford: Oxford University Press, 1996)

Aquinas, Thomas, *Summa Theologiae I*, q.12, a.12, ad.1: https://www.newadvent.org/summa/1012.htm#article12

Artaud, Antonin, quoted in Jean-Jacques Lecercle, *Philosophy through the Looking Glass: Language, Nonsense, Desire* (London: Hutchinson, 1985)

Augustine, *City of God*, translated by Henry Bettenson (London: Penguin, 2003)
—— *Sermones, Patrologiae Cursus Completus, series latina* (Paris: Migne, 1844-1864) vol. 38
—— *The Trinity*, translated by Edmund Hill, O.P. (Brooklyn, New York: New City, 1991)

Austen, Jane, *Emma* (London: Dent, 1980)

Saint Benedict, *The Rule of Saint Benedict*, translated by Caroline White (London: Penguin, 2008)

Boccaccio, *The Decameron*, translated by G. H. McWilliam (London: Penguin, 1995)

Broadley, Margaret, *Patients Come First: Nursing at 'The London' Between the Two World Wars* (London: The London Hospital Special Trustees, 1980)

Buchan, John, *Witch Wood* (London: Hodder and Stoughton, 1927. Reprinted 1941)

Carroll, Lewis, *Through the Looking Glass* (London: The Folio Society, 1962)

Cather, Willa, *O Pioneers!* (London: Penguin, 2018)

Cavell, Stanley, *The World Viewed: Reflections on the Ontology of Film*, enlarged edition. (Cambridge, MA: Harvard University Press, 1979)

Charlemagne, "Epistola de Litteris Colendis" https://sourcebooks. fordham.edu/source/carol-baugulf.asp

Chesterton, G.K., *G.K. Chesterton, An Anthology* (Oxford: Oxford University Press, 1957)

Chrétien de Troyes, "The Knight with the Lion (Yvain)' in Chrétien de Troyes, *Arthurian Romances*, translated by William Kibler (London: Penguin, 1991)

Dante, *The Divine Comedy* translated by C. H. Sisson (Oxford: Oxford University Press, 2008)

Deleuze, Gilles, *Difference and Repetition,* translated by Paul Patton (London: Bloomsbury, 2014)
—— *Logic of Sense,* translated by Constantin V. Boundas, Mark Lester and Charles J. Stivale (London and New York: Bloomsbury, 2015)

Dickens, Charles, *Pickwick Papers* (London: Penguin, 1999)

Dostoevsky, Fyodor, *The Brothers Karamazov*, translated by David Magarshack (Harmondsworth: Penguin, 1958)

Douglas, Mary, *Purity and Danger* (Abingdon: Routledge Classics, 2002)

Eliade, Mircea, *A History of Religious Ideas*, vol.1, translated by Willard R. Trask (Chicago: Chicago University Press, 1981)

Eliot, George, *Middlemarch* (Oxford: Oxford University Press, 1988)
—— *Scenes of Clerical Life* (London: Penguin, 1998)

Eriugena, John Scottus, *Praefatio Joannis Scoti versio Ambigorum S. Maximi in Patrologiae Cursus Completus, series latina* (Paris: Migne, 1844–1864) vol.122

Flecker, James Elroy, *The Golden Journey to Samarkand.* (United Kingdom: M. Secker, 1915)

Frost, Robert, *The Collected Poems* (London: Vintage, 2013)

Frye, Northrop, *Anatomy of Criticism: Four Essays* (London: Penguin, 1990)

Gregory Nazianzen, *Oration* xiv in *Patrologiae Cursus Completus, series graeca* (Paris: Migne, 1857–1886) vol. 35

Gregory of Nyssa, *Catechetical Oration*, xxv in *Patrologiae Cursus Completus, series graeca* (Paris: Migne, 1857–1886) vol.45
—— *Contra Eunomium XII, Patrologiae Cursus Completus, series graeca* (Paris: Migne, 1857-1886) vol.45
—— *In Ecclesiasten* vii in *Patrologiae Cursus Completus, series graeca* (Paris: Migne, 1857-1886) vol.44
Guerric d'Igny, *The Christmas Sermons of Bl. Guerric of Igny*, translated by Sr. Rosa of Lima (Trappist, KY: Abbey of Gethsemani, 1959)
Hegel, G.W.F., *Lectures on the Philosophy of Religion. The Lectures of 1827*, edited by Peter C. Hodgson, translated by R.F. Brown, P.C. Hodgson, & J.M. Stewart (Berkeley: University of California Press, 1988)
Herbert, George, 'The Country Parson' in *The Complete English Works* (New York: Everyman, 1995)
—— 'The Elixir' in *The Complete English Works*
Heidegger, Martin, *Parmenides*, translated by Andre Schuwer and Richard Rojcewicz (Bloomington and Indianapolis: Indiana University Press, 1998)
Hobbes, Thomas, *Leviathan*, edited by Edwin Curley (Indianapolis/Cambridge: Hackett, 1994)
Hostetter, Eric and Howe, Thomas Noble (eds), *The Romano-British Villa at Castle Copse, Great Bedwyn*, (Bloomington: Indiana University press, 2005)
Hugo, Victor, *Les Misérables*, translated by Norman Denny (London: Penguin, 1982)
Hume, David, *An Enquiry Concerning Human Understanding* (Peru, Illinois: Open Court Trade and Academic, 1988)
—— *Dialogues Concerning Natural Religion* (London: Penguin, 1990)
Irenaeus, *Against Heresies* in *Ante-Nicene Fathers. Translations of The Writings of the Fathers down to A.D. 325 – Justin Martyr – Irenaeus* (Buffalo: The Christian Literature Publishing Co., 1885)
Julian of Norwich, *Revelations of Divine Love*, translated by Barry Windeatt (Oxford: Oxford University Press, 2015)
Kant, Immanuel, *Critique of Pure Reason*, translated by Norman Kemp Smith (London & Basingstoke: Macmillan, 1933)
Keats, John, *The Complete Poems* (London: Penguin, 1988)

Kierkegaard, Søren, 'The Concept of Irony' in *The Essential Kierkegaard*, edited by Howard V. Hong & Edna H. Hong (Princeton: Princeton University Press, 2000)

—— *Fear and Trembling*, translated by Alastair Hannay (London: Penguin, 1985)

—— 'Lily in the Field, Bird in the Air' in *The Essential Kierkegaard*, edited by Howard V. Hong & Edna H. Hong (Princeton: Princeton University Press, 2000)

Kipling, Rudyard, 'The Gardener' in *The Man Who Would be King: Selected Stories of Rudyard Kipling* (London: Penguin, 2011)

Kondo, Marie, *The Life-Changing Magic of Tidying*, translated by Cathy Hirano (London: Vermillion, 2014)

Kuhn, Thomas, *The Structure of Scientific Revolutions*, 3rd ed. (Chicago: University of Chicago Press, 1996)

Brother Lawrence, *The Practice of the Presence of God* (Oxford: Mowbray, 1980)

Lessing, Gotthold Ephraim, *Lessing: Philosophical and Theological Writings*, translated and edited by H.B Nisbet (Cambridge: Cambridge University Press, 2005)

MacKenna, Stephen, *Journal and Letters of Stephen MacKenna*, edited with a memoir by E.R. Dodds (London: Constable & Co., 1936)

Nietzsche, Friedrich, *Beyond Good and Evil*, translated by Marion Faber (Oxford: Oxford University Press, 1998)

—— *The Joyous Science*, translated by R. Kevin Hill (London: Penguin, 2018)

—— *Thus Spoke Zarathustra*, translated by Graham Parkes (Oxford: Oxford University Press, 2005)

—— *Twilight of the Idols, or How to Philosophize with a Hammer.*, tanslated by Duncan Large (Oxford: Oxford University Press, 1998)

Nygren, Anders, *Agape and Eros*, translated by Philip S. Watson (Chicago: Chicago University Press and London: SPCK, 1982)

Picard, Max, *The World of Silence*, translated by Stanley Godman (South Bend, Indiana: Regnery/Gateway, 1952)

Plato, *The Trial and Death of Socrates*, translated by F.J. Church (London: Macmillan, 1915)

—— *Theaetetus*, edited by Bernard Williams, translated by M.J.

Levett. Revised by Myles Burnyeat (Indianapolis/Cambridge: Hackett, 1992)

Plotinus, *The Enneads*, translated by Stephen MacKenna (London: Penguin, 1991)

Porphyry, *On Abstinence from Killing Animals,* translated by Gillian Clark (London: Duckworth, 2000)

Ruskin, John, *Praeterita* (New York: Everyman, 2005)

Sartre, Jean-Paul, *Being and Nothingness*, translated by Hazel E. Barnes (Abingdon: Routledge, 2003)

Traherne, Thomas, *Thomas Traherne, Poetry and Prose* (London: SPCK, 2000)

Vanstone, W. H., *Love's Endeavour, Love's Expense: The Response of Being to the Love of God* (London: Darton, Longman and Todd, 2007)
—— *The Stature of Waiting* (London: Darton, Longman and Todd, 1982)

Vasari, Giorgio, *Lives of the Artists*, Vol.1, translated by George Bull (London: Penguin, 1987)

Waugh, Evelyn, *Helena* (London: Penguin, 2011)

Weil, Simone, *Gravity and Grace*, translated by Emma Crawford and Mario von der Ruhr (London: Routledge, 2002)
—— *Waiting for God*, translated by Emma Craufurd (New York: Harper Perennial Modern Classics, 2009)

Whitlock, Ralph, *Wiltshire Folklore and Legends* (London: Robert Hale, 1992)

Whitman, Walt, *Leaves of Grass* (New York: Penguin Classics, 1986)

Williams, Margery, *The Original Velveteen Rabbit or How Toys Become Real* (London: Egmont, 1992)

Wisdom, John, 'Gods' in *Philosophy and Psycho-Analysis* (Oxford: Basil Blackwell, 1953)

Wittgenstein, Ludwig, *Culture and Value*, translated by Peter Winch (Chicago: Chicago University Press, 1984)

*The Wizard of Oz*, directed by Victor Fleming (1939; Los Angeles: Metro-Goldwyn-Mayer. Burbank, CA: Warner Home Video, 2014) DVD

Wordsworth, William, 'Ode on Intimations of Immortality from Recollections of Early Childhood' in *The Golden Treasury*, selected by Francis Turner Palgrave. (Oxford: Oxford University Press, 1964)